IMPLEMENTING THE LITERACY HOUR FOR PUPILS WITH LEARNING DIFFICULTIES

Second Edition

IMPLEMENTING

THE

LITERACY HOUR

FOR PUPILS WITH LEARNING DIFFICULTIES

SECOND EDITION

ANN BERGER
AND DENISE MORRIS

David Fulton Publishers
London

David Fulton Publishers Ltd
Ormond House, 26–27 Boswell Street, London WC1N 3JZ

First published in Great Britain in 1999 by David Fulton Publishers
Second Edition 2001

Note: The right of the authors to be identified as the authors of this work
has been asserted by them in accordance with the Copyright, Design and
Patents Act 1988.

British Library Cataloguing in Publication Data
A catalogue record for this book is available from the British Library

ISBN 1–85346–756–1

Typeset by Textype Typesetters, Cambridge
Printed in Great Britain by Bell and Bain Ltd, Glasgow

Contents

Preface

The National Literacy Strategy in Bristol for pupils with severe, complex and profound learning difficulties

QCA have recently produced revised curriculum guidance and new P levels for pupils at the earliest stages of learning. This second edition of Implementing the Literacy Hour for Pupils with Learning Difficulties links these new level descriptions to the pre-Reception objectives linked to the National Literacy Strategy. It also includes a case study that shows how this framework has been used to develop a scheme of work in an all age special school for pupils with severe, profound, and complex learning needs.

Bristol schools have been involved in the National Literacy Project since 1996 and teachers in our special schools became more interested in getting involved as they heard from other teachers that it had a positive effect for many pupils with special needs. It was clear from the outset that the framework would need adaptations for pupils with the most severe learning difficulties and as an Authority we were keen to be involved in supporting our schools with this. Schools did not want to have to interpret the guidance on their own as many had to do with the National Curriculum.

Within Bristol we have pupils with increasingly complex learning needs in our mainstream schools. We need to develop the specialisms of teachers in our special schools in teaching the literacy hour so that they are able to advise and support when these pupils are included within the mainstream environment.

Raising standards of literacy in our special schools is also a key area of Bristol City's Education Development Plan. The National Literacy Strategy has provided the means to focus on this area and ensure that our teachers have high expectations and the maximum number of pupils reach national standards of literacy.

In order to provide support for our schools, we appointed a specialist literacy consultant with extensive experience with pupils with severe, complex and profound learning difficulties and set up the project, which has resulted in this book.

A video and a specialist training pack can be purchased which helps teachers use the Scheme of Work in this book (see back cover for details).

Ann Berger
Bristol
May 2001

Acknowledgements

Many people have helped us to write this book. In particular we wish to thank all the staff and pupils of:

Kingsweston School
Claremont School
Briarwood School
Florence Brown School
New Fosseway School

Thank you also to Ayleen Driver, Curriculum Support Teacher for Information and Communication Technology who linked the Learning Objectives to particular software packages.

Part **1** The Literacy Hour

Background to the National Literacy Strategy

In September 1996 the Department for Education and Employment (DfEE) established the National Literacy Project. The main purpose of the project was to raise standards of literacy by:

- Improving the progress in literacy by expecting lessons to be planned systematically, and teaching and learning to be monitored and evaluated by head teachers, senior staff and governors.
- Setting clear expectations for each term.
- Improving the quality of teaching by focusing more time on whole-class instruction and management.

Pupils with severe, complex and profound learning difficulties are not expected to attain the standards laid down in the National Literacy Strategy. For them work on language development, communication skills (including signing), object and symbol recognition will continue to form the basis of their learning.

However special schools are expected to implement the National Literacy Strategy as far as is possible. The guidance to registered inspectors from OFSTED suggests that, so far as is suitable for the pupils, literacy lessons in special schools should be as close as possible to those in mainstream primary schools.

Teachers will need to apply their professional judgement to determine the extent to which they can apply the framework.

In addition teachers now need to apply the new curriculum guidance and P level assessment descriptors to whole class and individual plans.

OFSTED inspections will judge whether schools have applied the framework as far as is suitable. Schools therefore need to consider carefully the National Literacy Strategy (NLS). This book suggests adaptations which are suitable for pupils with severe, complex and profound learning difficulties both in special and mainstream schools.

How this book was developed

This book is part of a Bristol City Council Education initiative to raise attainment in literacy for pupils with severe, profound and complex learning difficulties. It stems from the belief that the NLS can support *all* pupils in their journey of acquiring literacy skills.

The NLS consists of two key elements:

1

- the literacy hour
- the framework of learning objectives (NLF)

Both require adaptation if they are to provide teachers of pupils with severe, profound and complex needs with sufficient guidance to plan and teach literacy effectively.

This book is based on two main principles:

1. All pupils will benefit from the literacy hour and it should be taught in all schools.
2. The NLF needs to be broken down into small steps in order that all pupils can access the learning objectives. These steps need to clarify the crucial importance of developing communication skills.

Principles which underpin this book

This book has been written to support the implementation of the literacy hour for pupils with severe, complex and profound learning difficulties. It may also be useful for mainstream teachers who plan for pupils with a wider range of learning difficulties. It may also be used for some pupils whose physical disabilities inhibit their language development and for pupils with autism whose difficulties in communication require a very structured, 'small steps' approach.

What do we mean by literacy?

The development of communication and listening skills is an essential step towards reading and writing for pupils with severe, complex and profound learning difficulties. Therefore communication and listening are a focus of this document in the early stages.

The NLS defines literacy as meaning essentially reading and writing. For pupils with severe, complex and profound learning difficulties the access to reading and writing is through the development of language and communication. The Bristol project incorporates many of the tools used to teach communication, speech and language to pupils with special needs. In addition it enables access to the NLS and allows pupils with special educational needs to be fully included in this major national initiative.

Many pupils with moderate or severe learning difficulties by the end of Year 6 can:

- read and write with some confidence;
- use a range of reading cues;
- use elements of the sound and spelling system to improve the accuracy of their reading and spelling;
- write legibly;
- have an interest in words and their meaning and a growing vocabulary;
- know a range of genres and be familiar with some of the ways in which narratives are structured through basic literacy ideas of setting, character and plot;

- use and be able to write some non-fiction texts;
- plan and draft, revise and edit their own writing;
- discuss their reading and writing;
- be interested in books and read with enjoyment;
- through reading and writing begin to develop their powers of imagination and invention.

Pupils with more profound, severe and complex learning difficulties may be able to:

- show an awareness of their surroundings and their belongings;
- develop an awareness of people and of past and present;
- show a knowledge of a range of vocabulary;
- understand the meaning of previously unknown words;
- listen and respond to stories and non-fiction texts;
- follow a story, indicating enjoyment and understanding;
- anticipate and join in repetitive and familiar stories;
- use a wide range of IT to access literature and non-fiction texts;
- read simple sentences using either words or symbols.

The Literacy Hour

The Literacy Hour is designed to provide a practical structure to enable teachers to deliver an hour of literacy per day.

The clock diagram (Figure 1.1) shows the approximate times to be allocated to different activities. There may be a need to vary times and allow greater flexibility for some classes. However the structure has proved successful in many different groups in the Bristol pilot project.

When a school is inspected the assumption will be that a school is using the NLS structure. If schools adapt this, they need to state clearly why this is so in either their English policy or their teaching and learning policy.

Most schools for pupils with severe, complex and profound learning difficulties are already using more than an hour a day to develop communication skills. However, schools now need to ensure that there is a clear focus on literacy instruction and that an appropriate amount of time is allocated specifically to teaching the steps towards the National Literacy Strategy Learning Objectives. Usually this will be at least one hour per day, in addition to the guidance on successful teaching in the NLS (p. 8).

Teachers of pupils with severe, complex and profound learning difficulties may need to continue to use:

- multi-sensory approaches;
- clearly defined teaching based on pupils' literacy targets;
- a range of communication aids.

The clock shown as Figure 1.1 emphasises the whole-class teaching for shared text and writing work, focused word work and the plenary. This needs to be interpreted flexibly to ensure it meets the needs of each individual class. Some schools have found it more effective to use the first 15 minutes for whole-class teaching in order to deploy the support most efficiently.

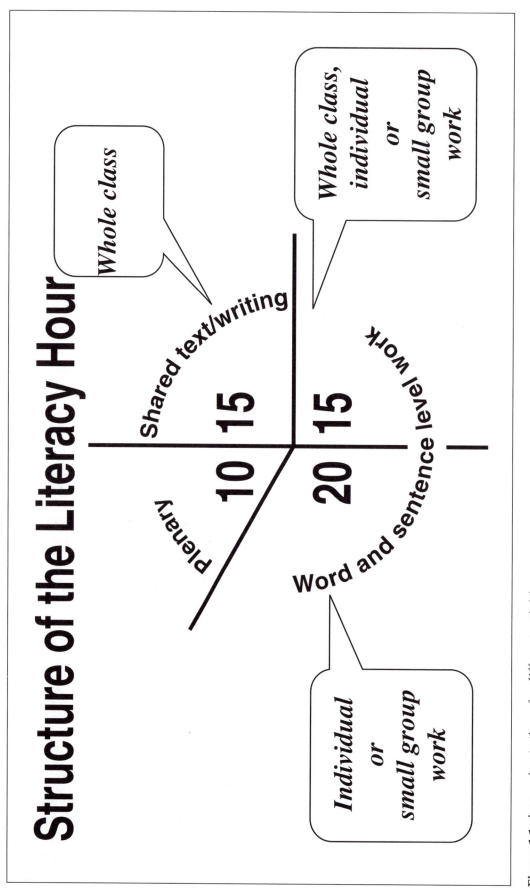

Figure 1.1 Approximate times for different activities

Whole-class teaching should always be based on demanding texts and challenging writing tasks to give confidence to the most and the least able and enable them to make progress. IEP work, in line with the Code of Practice on the Identification and Assessment of Special Educational Needs, should be planned to consolidate and support this progress.

Sometimes the shared text used may be based on the morning 'welcome' sessions and will include class photograph books and other personalised resources. A careful balance between fiction and non-fiction should be maintained.

The following timings have been successfully used in many of the pilot project schools.

The first part of the hour

This is a time when some pupils with SLD/PMLD will be developing their communication and listening skills through the range of interactive approaches suggested in this book. Many teachers will also include class topic books and pupils' own personal photograph books to enhance learning.

The second part of the hour – guided small group and one to one work on IEP literacy targets or whole phonics work

This section has three complementary purposes:

- To enable the teacher to teach at least one group or an individual, working on tasks related to their IEP literacy targets.
- To develop as far as possible independent working practices which may be supported by other adults. Few pupils with SLD/PMLD will be able to work independently for the full session. However activities such as practising writing, word/sentence matching and much of the tactile work for pupils with PMLD will enable some independent working styles to be developed over time.
- To teach phonics to the whole class where appropriate.

The plenary session with the whole class

This may be time for pupils to share their individual achievements and for the teacher to help pupils consolidate their learning and draw out the key learning intentions.

How to use the Scheme of Work in Part 3 of this book

The overall structure of the book follows the overall structure of the National Literacy Strategy framework with three interrelated strands: Word Level Work, Sentence Level Work and Text Level Work. The main emphasis at the early stages may be on word level work but pupils should have opportunities to learn words from texts and begin to build sentences from words.

Word level work	Sentence level work	Text level work
• Phonological awareness, phonics and spelling • Word recognition, graphic knowledge and spelling • Vocabulary extension • Handwriting	• Grammatical awareness	• Understanding of print • Reading comprehension • Writing composition

Measuring pupils' progress and setting targets

The DfEE and Qualifications and Curriculum Authority have redrafted guidance in March 2001 on setting targets for pupils with special needs, *Supporting the Target Setting Process*. They have produced eight 'level descriptions' for pupils working towards Level 1, as well as smaller steps for pupils at Levels 1 and 2. These will help schools assess what pupils know, understand and can do now, and will support schools in setting targets for pupils as part of their school improvement plans. Further support is available in *Assessing Pupils Using the P Levels* (2001).

Within the Scheme of Work in this book, each learning objective has been identified with a number 1 to 8. Teachers can choose objectives which match pupils' ability and also judge the progress being made using these levels. The numbers in the Scheme of Work match the 'P 1–8' levels for language and literacy. The QCA descriptors are designed for a 'best fit' approach. Some of the learning objectives are appropriate across two or three of the levels.

Each of the Reception Year learning objectives has been broken down into the small

Figure 1.2 A guided reading lesson with three Year 7 pupils

steps which lead to the achievement of those objectives. The numbering used is the same as in the NLF. However, the book is *not* planned in terms or age-related years but in steps towards *each* National Literacy Strategy Learning Objective. Some examples of activities relating to each step are included. These can be used to develop pupils' skills and understanding. Each step is identified in line with the QCA pre-Level 1 descriptors. For example W.L. P3 1.1 is the Word Level Objective 1.1 from the NLF. Interrelationships and links across the Learning Objectives are indicated to allow cross-referencing and blocking of work (see the following example).

WORD LEVEL: PHONOLOGICAL AWARENESS, PHONICS AND SPELLING
(*Note.* In the 'Suggested books' sections, an asterisk indicates a book suitable for older children.)

W.L. YR: LO 1.1

To understand and be able to rhyme through recognising, exploring and working with rhyming patterns.

See also: W.L. YR: LO 1.2; W.L. Yr 1 Term 1: LO 1

Part **2** Planning for the Literacy Hour

Long-term planning

Part 2 of this book deals with planning for the literacy hour for pupils with severe, complex and profound learning difficulties.

What should I teach?

1. The Scheme of Work

Part 3 provides a Scheme of Work, which can be used or adapted to form the school's long-term plan. It describes the structured steps towards achieving the objectives in the National Literacy Strategy. P1 is always the first level of experience and the final small step leads directly to the learning objective of the NLS. It also makes suggestions of activities to enable pupils to achieve these steps. Appropriate books and IT packages are also included for each objective. Each step has been referenced to the Qualifications and Curriculum Authority 'P' levels scale (2001) to support teachers in using the framework for assessment. (See the following example, Figure 2.1.)

WORD LEVEL: PHONOLOGICAL AWARENESS, PHONICS AND SPELLING

W.L. YR: LO 1.1

To understand and be able to rhyme through recognising, exploring and working with rhyming patterns.

See also: W.L. YR: LO 1.2; W.L. Yr 1 Term 1: LO 1

Levels	Learning Objectives/Targets	Activities/Strategies
P1	i) Encounters and experiences repetitive nursery rhymes as adult reads/sings, ensuring focus on awareness. Pupils may show simple reflex action, startled response. ii) Shows emerging awareness of activities by beginning to focus attention for short periods. They may give intermittent reactions to stimuli.	Teacher reads and re-reads simple nursery rhymes, finger rhymes, with puppets including big arm puppets. Large books, action rhymes. Pupils listen to music, Nursery Rhyme tapes. Adults focus on rhythm particularly for pupils with sensory impairment.
P2	i) Responds consistently to adult and to repetitive nursery rhymes by smiling or body movement or vocalisation. ii) Recognises familiar adult and responds proactively to activities by reaching out to touch, follows with eyes and cooperates in simple communication games.	Adult reads/enacts a familiar rhyme emphasising the rhyming words and prompts with question to elicit response or pauses with gesture to encourage response.

P3	i) Requests familiar activities, rhymes and songs by communicating preference in some way. Explores puppets and toys used as part of rhyming activities. ii) Anticipates what might happen next, in familiar rhymes and songs through body, facial movements. Vocalises at appropriate points in simple rhymes.	Adult reads/tells a familiar rhyme, and encourages pupils to anticipate what comes next by pausing and encouraging participation in some way. Puppets and toys as part of session will help exploration and anticipation.
P4	Shows interest in continuation of familiar rhymes and songs by body or facial movements, or by vocalising or signing 'more'/'again'. Initiates repetition and begins to copy sounds and rhyming words. Handles simple rhyme books and shows interest in trying to turn pages.	Adult uses rhyme with strong rhythm and teaches pupils to clap, bang, gesture in time to the rhythm. Adult encourages pupils to ask for 'more'.
P5	Joins in with aspects of familiar and favourite rhymes and songs, and complete a line such as 'Humpty Dumpty sat on the . . .' through words, signs or symbols. Finds simple pictures to go with rhymes such as Humpty Dumpty.	Adult sings or reads many familiar rhymes and songs encouraging pupils to complete as much as possible.
P6	Shows understanding that some words sound the same, e.g. wall/fall; men/ten by calling out/pointing/ facial or body movements. Begins to predict a rhyming word. Chooses favourite rhyme book.	Adult reads stories/rhymes with clear rhyming words, stressing these and helping pupils to identify those that rhyme by pointing/calling out. In small groups, pupils and adults work together to find rhyming words in poems, rhymes and stories.
P7	Finds words that sound the same in songs, rhymes, text and poems, by listening to the adult read or by reading/looking at the text themselves. Follows printed rhyme as adult reads.	Adults might read large rhyming text while pupils join in where they can and point out/underline/ indicate the words that sound the same.
P8	Adds a rhyming word to a partially completed rhyme. Uses a growing vocabulary to develop rhyming skills.	In small groups or 1:1, pupils work with adults to complete rhymes by adding one or more rhyming words.

Suggested books, other resources

Rhyme and analogy activity software: Sherston.

The Pig That Learned To Jig by Alan Trussell-Cullen, Pub: Wonder World Big Books, Badger Publishing. ISBN 185880 1931.

* *A World War II Anthology* selected by Wendy Body; Pelican Big Book, Pub: Longman. ISBN 0582 333830 (Large) 0582 337518 (Small).

Puppets. Tapes.

Figure 2.1

2. Summary of the range of work from Reception Year to Key Stage 3

In addition, the NLS defines the range of work that should be covered during the primary years. As shown below this has been reviewed and adapted to ensure good balance and breadth across the full range of genres. It is not term related but divided into five broad bands and includes a range for older pupils through KS3:

- Early Years/Reception
- Infant/Key Stage 1
- Lower Junior/Years 3/4
- Upper Juniors/Years 5/6
- Older pupils/Year 7+

EARLY YEARS/RECEPTION
Fiction and Poetry   A wide variety of traditional, nursery and modern rhymes, chants, action verses, poetry and stories with predictable structures and patterned language.
Non-fiction   Simple non-fiction texts, including recounts.

INFANT/KEY STAGE 1

Fiction and Poetry
 Stories with familiar settings:
     Stories and rhymes with predictable and repetitive patterns.
     Traditional stories and rhymes.
     Fairy stories.
     Stories and poems with familiar, predictable and patterned language from a range of
     cultures, including playground chants, action verses and rhymes.
     Plays.
     Stories about fantasy worlds.
     Poems with patterned and predictable structures.
     A variety of poems on similar themes.

Non-fiction   Signs, labels, captions, lists, instructions.   Information texts, including non-chronological reports.   Simple dictionaries.   Information texts including recounts of observations, visits, events.

LOWER JUNIORS/YEARS 3/4
Fiction and Poetry   Stories and a variety of poems with familiar settings.   Traditional stories; stories and poems from other cultures.   Stories and poems with predictable and patterned language.   Poems by significant children's poets.   Extended stories.   Stories by significant children's authors.   Different stories by the same author; texts with language play (e.g. riddles, tongue-twisters, humourous verse and stories).
Non-fiction   Instructions.   Dictionaries, glossaries, indexes and other alphabetically ordered texts.   Explanations.   Information texts including non-chronological reports.

UPPER JUNIORS/YEARS 5/6

Fiction and Poetry
Stories with familiar settings.
Plays.
Poems based on observation and the senses.
Shape poems.
Myths, legends, fables, parables.
Traditional stories, stories with related themes.
Oral and performance poetry from different cultures.
Adventure and mystery stories.
Stories by the same author.
Humorous poetry and poetry that plays with language, word puzzles, puns, riddles.

Non-fiction
Information texts on topics of interest.
Non-chronological reports.
Thesauruses, dictionaries.
Instructions.
Dictionaries without illustrations, thesauruses.
Letters written for a range of purposes: to recount, explain, enquire, congratulate, complain.
Alphabetical texts, directories, encyclopaedias, indexes.

OLDER PUPILS/YEAR 7+

Fiction and Poetry
Historical stories and short novels.
Play scripts.
Poems based on common themes (e.g. space, school, animals, families, feelings, viewpoints).
Classic fiction, poetry and drama by long established authors, including where appropriate, study of elements of a Shakespeare play.
Stories/novels about imagined worlds: science fiction, fantasy adventures.
Stories in series.
Classic and modern poetry, including poems from different cultures and times.
Stories/short novels, etc., that raise issues (e.g. bullying, bereavement, injustice).
Stories by the same author.
Stories from other cultures.
Range of poetry in different forms (e.g. haiku, cinquain, couplets, lists, thin poems, alphabets, conversations, monologues, syllabics, prayers, epitaphs, songs, rhyming forms and free verse).

Non-fiction
A range of text-types from reports and articles in newspapers and magazines.
Instructions.
Information texts on same or similar themes.
Explanations.
Persuasive writing: adverts, circulars, flyers.
Discussion texts: debates, editorials.
Information texts linked to other curricular areas.

Medium-term planning: a case study

When should I teach it?

The following case study shows how teachers at New Fosseway School developed their own scheme of work using this framework as a basis. They have identified texts for each key stage and have monitored coverage to ensure breadth and balance.

New Fosseway School is a school for pupils with severe learning difficulties many of whom work at levels between P1–P8. The following scheme of work has been developed to ensure breadth and balance, incorporating the National Literacy Strategy for pupils at KS1, 2 and 3.

Continuous units of work for Speaking and Listening enable pupils to benefit from a progressive range of activities as they move through the school. Aspects of drama are included, to enable entitlement for older pupils through KS3.

Guidance on the range of work at the different key stages is offered on pages 19 and 20, and include texts relevant to older pupils as well as younger ones. Some examples of monitoring the genre for each area are included on pages 21–23, as well as the monitoring of the balance of objectives taught as part of a topic. Figure 2.2 (see p. 25) shows an example of a half-termly plan.

This is just one way that a school has used this scheme of work to plan a broad, balanced and relevant literacy curriculum across the key stages.

A CASE STUDY
ENGLISH SCHEME OF WORK
Continuous Units of Work for SPEAKING AND LISTENING

ENGLISH: Speaking and Listening

P o S	Suggested Activities	Resources	Assessment Opportunities
• Developing awareness of sounds.	• Join in songs/rhymes featuring pupils' names, specific to activities.	Key objects – Objects of reference Songs Mirrors Bubbles Surprise toys Puppets Telephone Balloons Photographs Sensory stimulation material	• To which people and events do pupils react?
• Distinguishing between sounds.	• React to people and events within the environment.	Shaving foam Hats and other dressing-up clothes Cookery equipment	
• Reacting to sounds, e.g. head turning.	• Search for a sound source.	Tapes player/recorders Tapes TV/radio/video Musical instruments	• Which sounds do pupils show an interest in?
• Responding appropriately to sounds, e.g. smiling, crying.	• Join in anticipation games, e.g. round and round the garden; ready, steady, go.	Computer – cause and effect programme Toys	
• Imitating sounds.	• Imitate simple sounds, e.g. clapping.	Drink/dinner/snacks Home Creative equipment	
• Making sounds and babbling.	• Vocalise to self, reflections, people, music, etc.	Library Light Stimulation Room Ballpool	• What sounds do pupils make?
• Making recognisable sounds.	• Make different sounds to indicate hunger, distress, pleasure.	Dining hall Book Corner Derbyshire Language Scheme	
• Beginning to develop own verbal communication.	• Join in parallel play with adults; adults react to communicative behaviour. Use a dialogue of sound/action with adults.	Makaton signs/symbols Sound lotto games LDA and games Language master	
• Responding to some words, e.g. own name, 'dinner', 'drink', 'home time'.	• Signal, gesture or vocalise intentionally.	Big Mac Tapes – songs, stories, rhymes, raps Telephone	
• Responding to simple instructions, e.g. 'sit down', 'get your coat'.	• Join in games giving instructions, e.g. Simon Says	Recipes/Shopping lists Maps Visitors	
• Communicating by any means: reflexes, facial expression, eye-pointing, vocalisation, actions, gestures, signs.	• Join in hide/find, appear/disappear games.		
• Experiencing opportunities to make choices.	• Express real choices, needs or preferences, e.g. at drinks time.		• What things do pupils choose between?

ENGLISH: Speaking and Listening

P o S	Suggested Activities	Resources	Assessment Opportunities
• Working with others.	• Use an adult to gain an object.	PECS Books Magazines Newspapers Makaton symbol book Masks Pupil profiles ROA	• Which words/signs do pupils use?
• Turn taking.	• Take turns in social games, e.g. peek-a-boo.		
• Developing verbal communication – single words or signs relating to objects, people or events – cause and effect – sense of sequence.	• 'Show me what you want'. • Comment on or request disappearance of person/object. • Communicate not wanting an object, person or event or cessation of activity. • Comment on position or spatial relationship between objects, persons, events.		
• Increasing vocabulary of words and/or signs.	• Convey a relationship between an object or person and oneself or others, e.g. point to or vocalise self when asked whose coat is this?		
• Developing verbal language: – describing objects, events and people – expressing feelings in words – having fun with language.	• Talk about people in our lives. • Discuss healthy, unhealthy eating. • Talk about what causes happiness, sadness, worry, etc. • Make up silly rhymes, songs, raps, etc.		
• Imaginative play and role playing involving language.	• Take part in creating drama, role play, e.g. cooking, shopping, keeping safe.		
• Listening for meaning.	• Follow rules in group game.		
• Answering questions.	• Answer questions, e.g. about family, keeping safe.		• Can pupils answer questions – what? where? who? why? when?
• Gaining and holding attention of listener.	• Initiate conversation, e.g. to express, a need.		
• Developing clarity of speech.	• Use 2 and 3 element utterances, expand verbs.		

ENGLISH: Speaking and Listening

P o S	Suggested Activities	Resources	Assessment Opportunities
• Asking questions.	• Take turns, e.g. telling news, playing memory games.		• What sort of questions do pupils ask?
• Development of appropriate timing of contributions to discussons/conversations.			• Can pupils converse – taking turns to listen and respond to what speak and respond to what others say?
• Giving simple explanations, information and instructions.	• Talk about for example, own work, ways of helping others, keeping safe.		
• Adjusting language to suit audience, context and purpose.	• Act out simple story, make up a story, tell a joke.		• How do pupils vary their language?
• Perceive the relevance of others' contributions.	• Know who may be able to answer certain questions.		– with teachers?
			– with parents?
			– with friends?
• Understanding others' feelings/opinions.	• Be able to agree, disagree with another person.		– in public (assembly)?
• Developing clarity of argument, powers of recall and prediction.	• Hypothesise and predict about possible answers to questions.		– one-to-one?
• Reasoned discussions.	• Think about a question asked and if answer unknown, seek answer elsewhere.		
• Adjusting and adapting views.	• Attempt to solve problem situations set up by adult, e.g. what to do to develop a film.		

ENGLISH SCHEME OF WORK
Continuous Units of Work for READING AND WRITING

LITERACY: Word Level

P o S	Suggested Activities	Resources	Assessment Opportunities
Learning objectives from YR of NLS are broken down in BLS (Bristol Literacy Scheme).			
• Hearing and identifying initial sounds in words W.L. YR: LO 2.1.	• Listening games, e.g. I Spy. • Reading stories and poems. • Find own book, coat peg, picture.	General basic classroom resources.	• Which sounds do pupils identify?
• Writing letters in response to sounds W.L. YR: LO 2.4 and 8.	• Write initial letters of words. • Write own name on work. • Shopping lists. • Telephone messages. • Diaries and newsbooks. • Practice writing name, address and phone number.	Name cards.	• Which letters can pupils produce?
• Reading a range of familiar words W.L. YR: LO 5, 6 and 7.	• Captions for pictures, photographs. • Landmarks and labels around school. • Sight vocabulary from Sunshine Reading Scheme. • Social sight vocabulary. • Use word books and lists and dictionaries.		• Which words can pupils read?
• Developing a style of handwriting. W.L. YR: LO 12, 13 and 14.	• Making marks in sand, paint, etc. • Tracing. • Copying over and under model. • Tracks and mazes. • Patterns.	Mark making materials.	
• Visual discrimination.	• Matching objects, pictures. • Picking out detail from pictures. • Matching letters, words. • Picking set letters, words.		

LITERACY: Sentence Level

P o S	Suggested Activities	Resources	Assessment Opportunities
Learning objectives from YR of NLS are broken down in BLS.			
• Using capital letters. S.L. YR: LO 4.	• Find own name from a list of names. • Recognise that, e.g. R and r sound the same but capitals are used for names. • Use upper and lower case letters on computer keyboard.	Name cards. Symbol cards. Computers. Word books with upper and lower case letters.	• Can pupils read and write their own names?
• Using past tense.	• Talk about events which took place . . . yesterday, last week, Christmas time, etc. • Journals and newsbooks.		
• Answering and asking questions.	• Progression of questions from 'What is this?' to 'What will happen if?' and more complex question structure.	Basic classroom resources.	• What level of questioning does the pupil respond to?
• Sequencing.	• Ordering from left to right. • Talk about where to start reading (top of page) and where to finish (bottom of page). • Turn pages of book. • Sequence pictures to make a story. • Sequence own ideas, e.g. 'We'll do this first, then this and finish with this'.	Tracks. Picture books. Comic strips. LDA cards.	• How many events/pictures can pupils sequence?

LITERACY: Text Level

P o S	Suggested Activities	Resources	Assessment Opportunities
• Re-reading, reciting and re-telling stories. T.L. YR: LO 2, 3, 4, 5, 6, 7, 8, 9, 10.	• Recite rhymes and stories which pupils know well. • Anticipate words or phrases. • Join in with parts of stories which are repeated several times. • Act out stories or parts of stories.	General classroom resources.	• Can pupils re-tell stories?
• Reading comprehension. T.L. YR: LO 2, 3, 4, 5, 6, 7, 8, 9, 10.	• Talk about story language, e.g. 'Once upon a time', 'A long time ago'. • Find some familiar words in a story. • Answer questions on a story. • Read different versions of a traditional story and listen to a tape, watch a video if available. • Compare the endings of stories, e.g. happy/sad, funny/scary.	Literacy resources.	• Do pupils understand what is read to them? At what level?
• Writing composition. T.L. YR: LO 12, 13, 14, 15.	• Write labels and captions. • Write own name with a variety of mark making materials. • Dictate a story into a tape recorder. • Write greetings cards, shopping lists. • Home area play, e.g. doctor's prescriptions, telephone messages. • Write own news in journals. • Write own sentences for class story.	Mark making materials.	• Do pupils attempt to write their own compositions?

ENGLISH SCHEME OF WORK GUIDANCE FOR LITERACY

1) General Statement
2) Range of Work
3) Technical Vocabulary List
4) Suggested Texts

---

1) Reading and Writing (Literacy)

At Key Stages 1, 2 and 3 pupils follow programmes of study detailed in 'Implementing the Literacy Hour for Pupils with Learning Difficulties' and 'The National Literacy Strategy'.

At Key Stage 3 and in post-16 groups literacy is included in the core skill of communication. Elements of the National Literacy Strategy and the Bristol Scheme of Work are included where appropriate.

---

2) Range of Work
Key Stage 1 and lower Key Stage 2

At least	3 simple stories	Traditional nursery stories
		Stories with predictable structures and patterned language
		Fairy/fantasy stories
	2 non-fiction	Signs, labels, captions, lists, instructions, information texts
		Recounts of visits, events, observations
	4 poems	nursery rhymes
		modern rhymes
		chants
		action verses
		To be covered in a year

Upper Key Stage 2

At least	4 stories	Stories with familiar settings
		Traditional stories
		Stories from other cultures
		Different stories by the same author
		Adventure and mystery stories
		Letters
		Stories which voice issues, e.g. bullying.
	4 non-fiction	Information texts including encyclopedias
		Glossaries
		Indexes
		Instructions
		Alphabetical texts
		Adverts
	4 poems	Humorous verses, riddles, tongue-twisters
		Poetry that plays with language
		Range of poetry in different forms, e.g. conversations, couplets, songs, free verse.
	2 myths/legends	Aesop's Fables, Greek and Roman myths
		To be covered in a year

Key Stage 3

At least	6 stories	Sci-fi fantasy adventures
		Stories from other cultures and traditions
	1 novel	
	1 longer established story	Classics, e.g. Treasure Island
	1 play	Adaptation of part of a Shakespeare play
	4 non-fiction	Adverts, circulars, fliers
		Newspapers, magazines
		Dictionaries
		Letters, leaflets, brochures
		Reference texts
		Diaries and journals, e.g. Anne Frank
		Autobiographies, biographies

Range of Work cont.

	6 poems	Range of poetry in different forms
		Humorous poetry
		Puns, riddles, word puzzles
		Classic poetry
		Limericks, Kennings
		To be covered in a year

Key Stage 4 and Post-16

At least	2 stories	Myths and legends. Stories from other cultures and traditions, mysteries, historical, humour, sci-fi. Stories which include real life situations, e.g. Strangers in the Fog
	2 novels or longer stories	Classics, e.g. Christmas Carol
		Roald Dahl
	1 play	Adaptation of classics on film and TV
		Shakespeare play
	10 non-fiction	Results of visits, events, activities
		News reports
		Instructional texts – rules, recipes, directions, instructions
		Non-chronological writing
		Letters, Diaries, Dictionaries
		Posters, Notices
		Leaflets, Public information
		Advertisements, Reference texts
	2 poems	Limericks, riddles
		Longer classic poetry
		Shape poetry
		To be covered in a year

3) Technical Vocabulary List
Key Stage 1 and lower Key Stage 2

Word	Text	Sentence
Word	Book	
Letter	Beginning	
Sounds	End	
First sound	Page	
	Story	
	Poem	

Upper Key Stage 2

Word	Text	Sentence
Alphabet	Author	Capital letter
End sound	Title	Full stop
Middle sound	Label	Question mark
	Cover line	Sentence
	List	Speech marks
	Signs	
	Myth	
	Legend	
	Encyclopedia	

Key Stage 3

Word	Text	Sentence
Plural	Contents	Comma
Vowel	Index	Punctuation
Consonant	Dictionary	
Alphabetical order	Fiction	
	Non-fiction	
	Play	
	Character	
	Fact	

Technical Vocabulary List cont.

Sense/nonsense
Riddle
Tongue-twister
Verse
Plot
Audience
Novel
Myth
Legend

Key Stage 4 and Post-16

Word	**Text**	**Sentence**
Lower case	Rhyme	Bold print
Upper case	Instruction	Exclamation mark
Syllable	Report	
Pun	Fact	
Slang	Heading	
	Notes	
	Sequence	
	Traditional story	
	Opinion	
	Autobiography	
	Narrator	

4) Suggested Texts for Middle School Topics
Topic: How Things Work

Title	Author	Genre
The wheels on the bus JJ and the Washing Machine	Poetry/Rhyme Susan Field	Fiction
Iron Man Mrs Armitage on Wheels What Machine am I? My Robot Machines	Ted Hughes Quentin Blake } Karen King Child Education/ Infant Projects	Fiction Fiction Poetry
Jo Jo and the Robot Do Wacky Do	Joy Cowley Joy Cowley	Fiction Poetry

Topic: Water

Title	Author	Genre
Harry by the Sea The Beast in the Bath Tub Storm Boy	Gene Zion Kathleen Stevens Paul Owen Lewis	Fiction Fiction Fiction
1, 2, 3 Off to the Sea Turtle and Crane	Big book Wendy Body Big book S Cullimore	Rhyme Re-told story/legend
Water Tap	Made up Poetry/made up	

Topic: Senses

Title	Author	Genre
The Gingerbread Man Not Now Bernard Farmer Duck	Big Book Big Book Big Book	Fiction Fiction Fiction
Boo The Giant Jam Sandwich Five Minutes Peace	Colin McNaughton John Vernon Lord Jill Murphy	Fiction Rhyme Fiction
Let's Make Music What Can You See? Diwali books Chanukah story	Big Book Big Book Wendy Body	Rhyme Rhyme Non-fiction Non-fiction
The Wind Blew From Head to Toe One Snowy Night	Nick Butterworth	Fiction Fiction Fiction
The Big Blue Whale A Christmas Carol (adapted!) Cloudland	Charles Dickens John Burringham	Non-fiction Fiction Fiction

Topic: Winter → Spring

Title	Author	Genre
The Little Red Hen Let's Make Music Outdoor Poems	Brenda Parks & Judith Smith Ron Bacon Selected by Wendy Body	Traditional tale Rhyme Poetry
Jack and the Beanstalk Weather Chinese New Year	First Discovery	Non-fiction Non-fiction
Penguin Small Jack and the Beanstalk	Mike Inkpen	Fiction Traditional tale
Winter Rap	Made up	Poetry/made up
Penguins in a Stew	Gerald Rose	Fiction

4) Suggested Texts for Upper School Topics
Topic: Health & Survival

Title	Author	Genre
Oliver Twist	Charles Dickens	Novel
Macbeth	William Shakespeare	Play
Healthy Eating		Non-fiction
My Body		Non-fiction
Health leaflets/posters		Non-fiction
World War 2 Anthology		Poetry
George's Marvellous Medicine	Roald Dahl	Longer story

Topic: Environment		
Title	**Author**	**Genre**
Diary of Anne Frank	Anne Frank	Autobiography
City Rhymes		Poetry
In the Dark Dark Wood		Traditional tale

Topic: World of Work		
Title	**Author**	**Genre**
The Night Train	W H Auden	Poetry

Topic: Sport & Leisure		
Title	**Author**	**Genre**
The Jabberwocky		
A Midsummer Nights Dream	William Shakespeare	Play

Topic: Community		
Title	**Author**	**Genre**
Aesop's Fables		Fables
Pantomine		Play

Short-term planning

How should I teach it?

> The more detailed weekly planning should focus on the teaching *process*. (National Literacy Strategy, p. 15)

For teachers of pupils with learning difficulties the focus will be on devising tasks, activities and strategies to teach individual pupils the literacy target or targets on their IEPs during the five hours of literacy each week. Teachers may also wish to design their own format to show these individual programmes more clearly. (See Figure 2.3.)

Figure 2.4 shows how a teacher has planned the literacy hour for a week.

Framework for an Individual Educational Plan

The steps towards the NLF Learning Objectives can be broken down into smaller targets and recorded in the blank right hand column (see following example). The completed page can then be used as the literacy IEP for that pupil. The framework can also be used for assessment purposes and to evaluate the pupil's progress.

W.L. YR: LO 1.1

To understand and be able to rhyme through recognising, exploring and working with rhyming patterns.

See also: W.L. YR: LO 1.2; W.L. Yr 1 Term 1: LO 1

Levels	Learning Objectives/Targets	Activities/Strategies	Assessment/IEP/Evaluation
P1	i) Encounters and experiences repetitive nursery rhymes as adult reads/sings, ensuring focus on awareness. Pupils may show simple reflex action, startled response. ii) Shows emerging awareness of activities by beginning to focus attention for short periods. They may give intermittent reactions to stimuli.	Teacher reads and re-reads simple nursery rhymes, finger rhymes, with puppets including big armpuppets. Large books, action rhymes. Pupils listen to music, Nursery Rhyme tapes. Adults focus on rhythm particularly for pupils with sensory impairment.	

Figure 2.2 Example of a half termly plan for a class of KS2 pupils in a school for pupils with severe learning difficulties

Date		Titles	TEXT Range	WORD LEVEL Continuous Work	WORD LEVEL LOs	WORD LEVEL Blocked Work	SENTENCE LEVEL Continuous Work	SENTENCE LEVEL LOs	SENTENCE LEVEL Blocked Work	TEXT LEVEL Continuous Work	TEXT LEVEL LOs	TEXT LEVEL Blocked Work
			fiction Makaton/Sunshine readers rhyme myth	Key words – s/s; Mak; names; vocab LO's 5–11 Handwriting/Fine motor LO's 12–14 L→R ordering – books/sequencing LO 3			Capital letters – names LO 4 Past tense – journals, ROA's LO 2 Questions based on text LO 1 1:1 written/spoken word LO 1.4 Re-read/tell LO 6, 7, 8, 12.5, 14 Handwriting LO 12.1, 12.2, 11.4 Story-structure LO 1.3, 5, 9			Journals, ROA's, books LO 12–3, 13, 11.3, 1.2, 12.4 Makaton scheme LO 1.1, 1.4 Cuso-reading LO 3, 2		
2.5 – 5.5	f	Planet of the monsters			YR 21–25 Yr 1 3, 5	Sounds – hear id.		LO2 tense	Past tense holidays journals		YR 12.3, 12.4	Composition – journals
8.5 – 12.5	m	Ulysses			YR 1 3, 5 YR 2.5	Sounds – hear id.		LO1	Questions based on text		YR 12.3, 12.4, 12.5	Composition – re-tell/ write
16.5 – 19.5					Yr 1 6	Sounds – hear id.		LO1	Questions based on text		YR 12.3, 12.4, 12.5	Composition – re-tell/ write
22.5 – 26.5	f	Hansel & Gretel			Yr 1 4.3, 1.2, 3.2	Sounds – alliteration		LO4	Capital letters in text/names		YR 13	Composition – plan
12.6 – 16.6	f	Mr. Grumpy's outing			YR 5, 8 Yr 1 7–9	Sight vocabulary – names, captions		LO4	Capital letters in text/names		YR 14	Composition – incl-ideas
19.6 – 23.6	f	Oi, get off our train			YR 6, 7, 9 Yr 1 10–12	Sight vocab – words banks		LO1	Sense of text		YR 14	Composition – incl-ideas
26.6 – 30.6	Rh	Grandma McGarvey			YR 1.1, 1.2 4.1, 4.2	Rhyme – patterns – levels, onset		LO2	Prediction/re-reading		YR 6, 10 Yr 14, 6	Rhyme
3.7 – 7.7	f	Me and my flying machine			Yr 1 1, 3, 5 YR 1.1, 1.2, 4.1, 4.2 Yr 1–1, 3, 5	Sounds – hear, id.		LO3	L→R ordering		YR 1.4, 11.5	Print (L→R)
10.7 – 14.7	f	Funnybones				Sounds – hear, id.		LO3	L→R ordering		YR 1.4, 11.4, 11.5	Print (L→R)
17.7 – 21.7	f	Princess Smarty-pants				Sounds – hear, id.		LO3	L→R ordering		YR 1.4, 11.4, 11.5	Print (L→R)

New Fosseway School
INDIVIDUAL EDUCATION PLAN

Name: KIMBERLEY FEBRY	Date to start: NOVEMBER 2001	Date to Review FEB 2002

To develop her use of symbols to communicate as part of PECS

Target 1: To use 5 PECS symbols in 1-1 setting and under classroom setting.	Strategy/Resources (what? how? who? when?): Play people, biscuit, drink, Lego, toilet. As part of literacy hour use with folder. Speech therapy sessions.
Date: 5/1 21/1 8/2	Comments/Evidence of Achievement: Uses 3 symbols consistently in wider setting. Will carry symbol file to lunch and use symbols. Uses 5 consistently. Uses 6 symbols consistently.

To look at and use photographs and symbols in choice making, timetable and literacy activities

Target 2: To use pictorial timetable and link photographs to activities.	Strategy/Resources (what? how? who? when?): Circle time timetable. Before each activity looking at photo.
Date: 5/1 8/1	Comments/Evidence of Achievement: Interested in photographs and links summary and bus to activities. Is able to identify photos and symbols with variety of activities.

Figure 2.3 Example of an individual education plan linked to the weekly plan

National Literacy Strategy
Weekly Plan
Name of School

Class: Year Group(s): Term: Week Beginning: Teacher:	Whole class – shared reading and writing	Whole class – phonics, spelling, vocabulary and grammar	Guided Group Tasks (reading or writing):	Guided Group Tasks (reading or writing): P1–2	Independent Group Tasks P3–4				Plenary
Mon	Ntikuma and the drum Year 5	Pupils listen to and join in with drum – beat rhythms		Play with different drums coactively if not independently					How do pupils respond to drums?
			T	T	—	OA	—		
Tues		Teacher chants '– has the drum' while beating the rhythm. Pupils beat drum independently		Loud/quiet drum sounds	Listen to fast/slow	From a selection of instruments, 'Give/ Show me the –'			How do pupils respond to tempo and dynamic of rhythm?
			T	T	—	OA	—	OA	
Wed		Teacher likes 2 symbols – drum and Ntikuma. 'Show me –'		T. plays drum behind or to side of P.	Match pictures/symbols to musical instrument				Do pupils recognise symbols?
			T	OA	—	OA	—	OA	
Thurs		Make a tape of drum rhythms to use as a cue for literacy hour this term		Walk around the school and outside. Drum in different places to hear the change in reverberation	Colour a picture of a drum (scribble over picture)	OA	—		Is mask making horizontal, circular, random?
			T	OA	—	OA	—		
Fri		Look at and listen to different kinds of drum		Make an intimate space (in text under practice) and listen to a tape of drum music (brass bands, African music, some music with drum beats)		OA	—		Do pupils show preferences in drum sounds, speed of rhythm etc?
			T	OA	—	OA	—		

Figure 2.4 Example of medium-term plan

National Literacy Strategy
Weekly Plan
Name of School

Class:
Year Group(s):
Term:
Week Beginning:
Teacher:

	Whole class – shared reading and writing	Whole class – phonics, spelling, vocabulary and grammar	Guided Group Tasks (reading or writing):	Guided Group Tasks (reading or writing): P5–6	Independent Group Tasks P7–8	1C–1B	1A–2C	Plenary
Mon	Ntikuma and the drum Year 5	T. taps out the rhythm of P's names on the drum. Pupils copy.		Find all the words in the story that start with 'd'	Match word cards and practice writing them	On a flip chart find and write all the words which start with d, m and t	Punctuate some sentences which the teacher has written without punctuation	Which words can the pupils read already?
			T	T	OA —	OA —	OA —	
Tues		Make a list of words from the story for classroom display and read together		Listen to different drum rhythms and try to copy them	T. rewrites the story as a flip chart following pupils' ideas	Play 'I Spy' using a page from the book	Make a list of words which rhyme with drum, bean etc.	Which rhythms can pupils copy?
			T	T	OA —	OA —	OA —	
Wed		Photocopy a page from the book. Blu-tack word cards to the picture as labels		Using 3 picture or symbols cards:- sequence the story	Make a sentence from individual word cards	Sequence word cards from the story in alphabetical order	Write some onomatopoeic words which sound like a drum.	Can pupils sequence picures? words? sentences?
			T	T	OA —	OA —	OA —	
Thurs		Look at the word 'drum'. Practice writing 'd' in the air. Each p. write the word on a white/black board		Match symbols to pictures from the story	Make a zigzag book with pictures and words from the story	Play word lotto using words from the text	'Spelling test' T. reads words from story. P. writes them down	Questioning from what is this? to what does Ntikuma feel like now?
			T	T	OA —	OA —	OA —	
Fri		Read the story but miss out some words for the pupils to complete		Draw a picture of part of the story and write a caption	Draw a picture and write a caption	Draw a picture and write a sentence	Write about why you like/don't like the book	Writing level and handwriting
			T	OA —	OA —	OA —	OA —	

Figure 2.4 (contd.)

Part 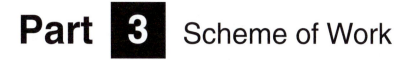 3 Scheme of Work

The framework for pupils with learning difficulties, including suggested activities and resources

A pupil working on W.L. YR: LO 13. To produce a controlled line which supports letter formation. Practising following a path with her finger and not straying into the garden.

Strand 1   Word Level Work: Reception

Phonics, spelling and vocabulary

PHONOLOGICAL AWARENESS, PHONICS AND SPELLING
Learning Objectives

WORD RECOGNITION, GRAPHIC KNOWLEDGE AND SPELLING
Learning Objectives

VOCABULARY EXTENSION
Learning Objectives

HANDWRITING
Learning Objectives

WORD LEVEL: PHONOLOGICAL AWARENESS, PHONICS AND SPELLING

W.L. YR: LO 1.1

To understand and be able to rhyme through recognising, exploring and working with rhyming patterns.

See also: W.L. YR: LO 1.2; W.L. Yr 1 Term 1: LO 1

Steps	Learning Objectives/Targets	Activities/Strategies	Assessment/IEP/Evaluation
P1	i) Encounters and experiences repetitive nursery rhymes as adult reads/sings, ensuring focus on rhythm to enable sensory awareness. Pupils may show simple reflex action, startled response. ii) Shows emerging awareness of activities by beginning to focus attention for short periods. They may give intermittent reactions to stimuli.	Teacher reads and re-reads simple nursery rhymes, finger rhymes, with puppets including big arm puppets. Large books, action rhymes. Pupils listen to music, Nursery Rhyme tapes. Adults focus on rhythm particularly for pupils with sensory impairment.	
P2	i) Responds consistently to adult and to repetitive nursery rhymes by smiling or body movement or vocalisation. ii) Recognises familiar adult and responds proactively to activities by reaching out to touch, follows with eyes and cooperates in simple communication games.	Adult reads/enacts a familiar rhyme emphasising the rhyming words and prompts with question to elicit response or pauses with gesture to encourage response.	
P3	i) Requests familiar activities, rhymes and songs by communicating preference in some way. Explores puppets and toys used as part of rhyming activities. ii) Anticipates what might happen next, in familiar rhymes and songs through body, facial movements. Vocalises at appropriate points in simple rhymes.	Adult reads/tells a familiar rhyme, and encourages pupils to anticipate what comes next by pausing and encouraging participation in some way. Puppets and toys as part of session will help exploration and anticipation.	
P4	Shows interest in continuation of familiar rhymes and songs by body or facial movements, or by vocalising or signing 'more'/'again'. Initiates repetition and begins to copy sounds and rhyming words. Handles simple rhyme books and shows interest in trying to turn pages.	Adult uses rhyme with strong rhythm and teaches pupils to clap, bang, gesture in time to the rhythm. Adult encourages pupils to ask for 'more'.	

Suggested books, other resources
Rhyme and analogy activity software: Sherston.
The Pig That Learned To Jig by Alan Trussell-Cullen. Pub: Wonder World Big Books, Badger Publishing. ISBN 185880 1931.
* *A World War II Anthology* selected by Wendy Body; Pelican Big Book. Pub: Longman. ISBN 0582 333830 (large) 0582 337518 (small).
Puppets. Tapes.

WORD LEVEL: PHONOLOGICAL AWARENESS, PHONICS AND SPELLING

W.L. YR: LO 1.1 *cont.*

To understand and be able to rhyme through recognising, exploring and working with rhyming patterns.

See also: W.L. YR: LO 1.2; W.L. Yr 1 Term 1: LO 1

Steps	Learning Objectives/Targets	Activities/Strategies	Assessment/IEP/Evaluation
P5	Joins in with aspects of familiar and favourite rhymes and songs, and completes a line such as 'Humpty Dumpty sat on the . . .' through words, signs or symbols. Finds simple pictures to go with rhymes such as Humpty Dumpty.	Adult sings or reads many familiar rhymes and songs encouraging pupils to complete as much as possible.	
P6	Shows understanding that some words sound the same, e.g. wall/fall; men/again by calling out/pointing/facial or body movements. Begins to predict a rhyming word. Chooses favourite rhyme book.	Adult reads stories/rhymes with clear rhyming words, stressing these and helping pupils to identify those that rhyme by pointing/calling out. In small groups, pupils and adults work together to find rhyming words in poems, rhymes and stories.	
P7	Finds words that sound the same in songs, rhymes, text and poems, by listening to the adult read or by reading/looking at the text themselves. Follows printed rhyme as adult reads.	Adults might read large rhyming text while pupils join in where they can and point out/underline/indicate the words that sound the same.	
P8	Adds a rhyming word to a partially completed rhyme. Uses a growing vocabulary to develop rhyming skills.	In small groups or 1:1, pupils work with adults to complete rhymes by adding one or more rhyming words.	

Suggested books, other resources
Rhyme and analogy activity software: Sherston.
The Pig That Learned To Jig by Alan Trussell-Cullen. Pub: Wonder World Big Books, Badger Publishing. ISBN 185880 1931.
* *A World War II Anthology* selected by Wendy Body; Pelican Big Book. Pub: Longman. ISBN 0582 333830 (large) 0582 337518 (small).
Puppets. Tapes.

WORD LEVEL: PHONOLOGICAL AWARENESS, PHONICS AND SPELLING

W.L. YR: LO 1.2

To understand and be able to rhyme through extending these patterns by analogy, generating new and invented words in speech and spelling.

See also: W.L. YR: LO 1.1; W.L. Yr 1 Term 1: LO 1

Steps	Learning Objectives/Targets	Activities/Strategies	Assessment/IEP/Evaluation
P1	i) Encounters and experiences repetitive rhyming songs and nursery rhymes with clear focus on rhythm as in 1.1. Shows reflex response to activities. ii) Focuses on adult for brief periods as rhythmic activities take place. Shows excitement at different instruments or rhythms.	Adults ensure wide range of rhythmic experiences using clapping, musical instruments and familiar rhymes and songs.	
P2	i) Responds consistently to adult reading repetitive nursery rhymes and songs by smiling/body movement/vocalisation and exploration of instruments. ii) Vocalises and/or gestures to communicate awareness of adult reading/singing/playing rhythms.	Adult reads and re-reads each line of known rhyme stressing the rhyme in each; musical experiences can be added to enhance understanding and enjoyment, e.g. clapping to the rhythm of the rhyme, or particularly clapping, or banging drum on the rhyming words.	
P3	i) Seeks attention in some way and tries to communicate as adult pauses during reading/singing of rhymes. ii) Anticipates what might happen next during the rhyming song or poem e.g. showing excitement and awareness that a rhyme has been missed out perhaps.	Adults read/sing very familiar rhymes and poems with appropriate silences and pauses to enable anticipation and expectation.	

Suggested books, other resources
Clicker with appropriate ready made or self made grid: Crick.
Queen of Hearts, Pub: Ginn. ISBN 0-602-28031-1.
See also *Jumbled, Tumbled Tales and Rhymes*, Pub: Ginn.
* *Along Came Greedy Cat* by Joy Cowley, Pub: Nelson. ISBN 017401 17537.
See also other books in 'Ready to Read Series'. Pub: Nelson.

WORD LEVEL: PHONOLOGICAL AWARENESS, PHONICS AND SPELLING

W.L. YR: LO 1.2 *cont.*

To understand and be able to rhyme through extending these patterns by analogy, generating new and invented words in speech and spelling.

See also: W.L. YR: LO 1.1; W.L. Yr 1 Term 1: LO 1

Steps	Learning Objectives/Targets	Activities/Strategies	Assessment/IEP/Evaluation
P4	Shows interest in continuation of familiar rhymes/songs by trying to vocalise/sign or indicate where adult has gone wrong, or where rhyming words have been missed out. Shows understanding of what comes next in familiar rhymes.	In small groups or individually, working with adult, pupils complete rhymes by vocalising or showing awareness in some way that the rhyme has not finished.	
P5	Joins in with some aspects of familiar rhymes and poems. Completes part of line in familiar rhyme such as 'Humpty Dumpty' through word/sign, etc.	In small groups, adult provides range of opportunities for pupils to complete rhymes.	
P6	Shows understanding of similar sounding words by finding one the same in familiar Rhymes, e.g. 'Humpty Dumpty sat on the Wall . . . what other word rhymes with wall?'	In small groups or individually pupils work with adults to find similar sounding words in large text stories/rhymes/poems.	
P7	Joins in with finding words that sound the same in less familiar rhymes and stories.	Increasing range of text as above.	
P8	Completes rhymes by adding own ideas for a rhyming word in a range of different Contexts.	Working individually where possible, pupils use large text/word cards/picture cards to find own ideas for rhyming words.	

Suggested books, other resources
Clicker software with appropriate ready made or self made grid: Crick.
Queen of Hearts. Pub: Ginn. ISBN 0-602-28031-1.
See also *Jumbled, Tumbled Tales and Rhymes*. Pub: Ginn.
* *Along Came Greedy Cat* by Joy Cowley. Pub: Nelson. ISBN 017401 17537.
See also other books in 'Ready to Read Series'. Pub: Nelson.

WORD LEVEL: PHONOLOGICAL AWARENESS, PHONICS AND SPELLING

W.L. YR: LO 2.1

Knowledge of grapheme/phoneme correspondences through hearing and identifying initial sounds in words.

See also: W.L. YR: LO 2.4, 2.5; W.L. Yr 1 Term 1: LO 3

Steps	Learning Objectives/Targets	Activities/Strategies	Assessment/IEP/Evaluation
P1	i) Encounters and experiences different sounds including musical instruments to enable breadth of experience of sounds. Startled on hearing or feeling sudden sounds. ii) Focuses on activities such as 'peek a boo' and may become excited.	Use of a range of musical games, toys, tapes, and voice and of listening/hearing programmes. To ensure that pupils hear/feel the rhythms and sounds. Peek-a-boo e.g. 'B b boo'.	
P2	i) Responds consistently in some way to different sounds and musical games through body movements, smiling, etc. ii) Knows when own name is called and begins to cooperate with responding at appropriate time.	Use of a range of listening games, especially music, and use of auditory discrimination activities, music, tapes, matching sound to object. To elicit a response of some kind, e.g. body movement, vocalisation, etc. Hello songs with name repetition.	
P3	i) Sustains attention for short periods during sound games. Looks and responds in some way. ii) Anticipates sounds, begins to know what comes next in familiar sequence. Begins to request particular sounds. Moves to the rhythm of some music.	Individual activity on sound lotto games and other practical sound activities such as sound box. Repetitive calling of pupils' names and praising response. Anticipation such as 'Jack in the box' with lots of adult vocalisation, e.g. 'Ready, steady Whoosh!'	
P4	Shows interest in continuing to hear and make different sounds, and in the names of other pupils as they are called. Tries to imitate and copy sounds. Obeys request to find objects with same sound.	Either in groups, or individually use familiar words, such as own name, to emphasise initial sound, then finding and listening to same sound at the beginning of different words. Sound lotto games. Daily calling of the register. Toys and instruments to explore and listen to: Cars to 'brum brum'. Trains to 'choo choo', etc.	

Suggested books, other resources
Clicker with appropriate ready made or self made grid: Crick.
Red Riding Hood by Stan Cullimore. Pub: Addison Wesley Longman Ltd. ISBN 0582 333458 (large) 0582 337526 (small)
* *Elmer* by David McKee. Pub: Anderson Press. ISBN 00992 65231.
Listening Resources, e.g. LDA. Sound LOTTO games. Tape recorders. Taped stories.

WORD LEVEL: PHONOLOGICAL AWARENESS, PHONICS AND SPELLING

W.L. YR: LO 2.1 *cont.*

Knowledge of grapheme/phoneme correspondences through hearing and identifying initial sounds in words.

See also: W.L. YR: LO 2.4, 2.5; W.L. Yr 1 Term 1: LO 3

Steps	Learning Objectives/Targets	Activities/Strategies	Assessment/IEP/Evaluation
P5	Joins in with repetition of same sounds such as copying adult banging drum/clapping. Joins in with helping to find own name card (picture/symbol or word).	In small groups pupils have opportunities to copy adult patterns with musical instruments; they use word and picture cards to find correct picture on request. They begin to play games in which they find objects beginning with own sound.	
P6	Understands that their own name is different from others, and begins to recognise other words with the same initial sound/letter when adult says it.	While listening to stories and rhymes pupils indicate when own initial sound is used. Games such as indicating when they hear their own sound, or another familiar one in a rhyme or story.	
P7	Joins in with finding a wider range of words with same initial letter/sound as own and begins to identify other familiar initial letters and sounds, e.g. some of the other pupils in the class as their names are called.	Opportunities to identify and make lists of things beginning with the same initial letter, e.g. Making collections e.g. a table with things beginning with 'b'. Adult repeatedly says the sound, e.g. 'b b ball' 'your turn . . . it's a . . .'	
P8	Identifies many different letter names and sounds, as adult reads or shows objects.	Range of games in small groups in which pupils find objects beginning with certain letters/sounds, e.g. 'Find me something beginning with B'. Eye-spy for example. Object/letter matching games.	

Suggested books, other resources
Clicker with appropriate ready made or self made grid: Crick.
Red Riding Hood by Stan Cullimore. Pub: Addison Wesley Longman Ltd. ISBN 0582 333458 (large) 0582 337526 (small)
* *Elmer* by David McKee. Pub: Anderson Press. ISBN 00992 65231.
Listening Resources, e.g. LDA. Sound LOTTO games. Tape recorders. Taped stories.

WORD LEVEL: PHONOLOGICAL AWARENESS, PHONICS AND SPELLING

W.L. YR: LO 2.2

Knowledge of grapheme/phoneme correspondences through reading letter(s) that represent(s) the sound(s).

See also: W.L. Yr 1 Term 1: LO 5

Steps	Learning Objectives/Targets	Activities/Strategies	Assessment/IEP/Evaluation
P1	As LO 2.1. Also encounters and experiences interaction with adult support to establish object constancy.	Individually pupils work with adults to experience a wide range of sensory activities such as visual/tactile/auditory toys which they are encouraged to touch/look at/and listen to.	
P2	i) Responds to familiar objects and people by looking/body movement/vocalisation. ii) Explores toys interactively as adult names them.	Activities as above but extended to more specific naming of objects by adult as pupil is encouraged to interact.	
P3	i) Participates in shared games to promote understanding of sounds. Sustains concentration in 'finding' games. ii) Anticipates activities and missing objects and begins to look for missing toys. Actively explores different media looking for objects begining with certain sounds.	Activities such as hiding toys under a cloth, encouraging searching while adult names, e.g. Find teddy. Where's teddy?' Encouraging anticipation of times in the day, e.g. dinner time/home time.	
P4	Shows interest in objects by looking and touching and playing and repeats name, begins to make simple signs for object. Responds to request to 'give me'. Shows understanding that different objects have different names, and begins to repeat initial sound by imitating.	Toy play with adults. Discussion with adults while looking at enlarged photographs of familiar (family) people.	

Suggested books, other resources
Clicker with appropriate ready made or self made grid: Crick
Letter Cluster Books: *Alphabet Starter*. Pub: Folens
Own name cards/symbols, photographs of self and family members, class words and class books.
Collection of objects beginning with relevant letter/sound.
Phonic cards, e.g. LDA/Early Learning Set/Alphabet Cards.

WORD LEVEL: PHONOLOGICAL AWARENESS, PHONICS AND SPELLING

W.L. YR: LO 2.2 *cont.*

Knowledge of grapheme/phoneme correspondences through reading letter(s) that represent(s) the sound(s).

See also: W.L. Yr 1 Term 1: LO 5

Steps	Learning Objectives/Targets	Activities/Strategies	Assessment/IEP/Evaluation
P5	Joins in with finding or looking at objects on request, and begins to recognise some simple photographs of familiar people, and pictures of familiar objects.	Toy play with a wide range of toys with adult support to name and encourage active participation, e.g. brushing doll's hair, putting cars in garage.	
P6	Shows understanding that things have names/labels and begins to use them appropriately to name objects and simple pictures either vocally or through signs/symbols/technology. Understands that own name begins with a certain letter (2.1).	Collections of pictures (perhaps linked to P5/6 2.1) which begin with the same letter, e.g. 'Let's collect all the toys beginning with t', 'Let's make a book of pictures of all the things beginning with t', etc.	
P7	Joins in with finding pictures that begin with a certain sound, and begins to link them with initial sounds that they hear (2.1) and to identify the written form of their own and some other familiar letters.	Opportunities for pupils to identify the written form of familiar letters/sounds within large text, including stories and rhymes. Everyday classroom activities such as finding name cards; job cards; named areas around the room, etc.	
P8	Continues to recognise an increasing number of letters that represent sounds.	As above, increasing the number of letters/sounds that pupils work with during their shared text and group times. Letter/sound snap and lotto games.	

Suggested books, other resources
Clicker with appropriate ready made or self made grid: Crick
Letter Cluster Books: *Alphabet Starter.* Pub: Folens
Own name cards/symbols, photographs of self and family members, class words and class books.
Collection of objects beginning with relevant letter/sound.
Phonic cards, e.g. LDA/Early Learning Set/Alphabet Cards.

WORD LEVEL: PHONOLOGICAL AWARENESS, PHONICS AND SPELLING

W.L. YR: LO 2.3

Knowledge of grapheme/phoneme correspondences through writing each letter in response to each sound.

See also: W.L. YR: LO 2.4, 2.5; W.L. Yr 1 Term 1: LO 6

Steps	Learning Objectives/Targets	Activities/Strategies	Assessment/IEP/Evaluation
P1	i) Encounters and experiences a range of sensory activities and toys with constant adult intervention to encourage a reaction. ii) Shows an emerging awareness of different textures and begins to focus on hands or objects covered in a texture.	Use of sensory environments to encourage tactile exploration of wide range of media, e.g. florescent paints, dough, sand water, etc. as well as toy play. Link with activities and programmes to improve hand function where possible, and/or switch operations.	
P2	i) Responds to multi-sensory experiences, particularly tactile objects by looking and feeling as adult names and supports. ii) Moves hands proactively showing a response to different textures. Imitates adult play with different media.	As above. With increasing adult intervention as responses occur.	
P3	i) Sustains concentration for short periods while exploring media. Vocalises responses to activities. ii) Anticipates tactile experiences by moving hands/fingers/body towards media and becoming excited as it is prepared.	As above. Adult encourages anticipation by continually saying 'are you ready, steady . . .', etc.	
P4	Explores actively to find objects hidden in dough, jelly, sand water, etc. Anticipates starting to explore by various body movements and vocalisations.	Activities to further improve hand function and coordination such as making hand and finger prints, picking up beads and small items, putting bricks in a tower and knocking them over (link to numeracy activities for early number work).	

Suggested books, other resources
Clicker with appropriate ready made or self made grid: Crick.
Letter Cluster books: *Alphabet starter*. Pub: Folens.
Range of tactile resources, e.g. sand tray, light pen, paint. Own name cards/symbols. Class words and class books.
Collection of objects from 2.2.

WORD LEVEL: PHONOLOGICAL AWARENESS, PHONICS AND SPELLING

W.L. YR: LO 2.3 *cont.*

Knowledge of grapheme/phoneme correspondences through writing each letter in response to each sound.

See also: W.L. YR: LO 2.4, 2.5; W.L. Yr 1 Term 1: LO 6

Steps	Learning Objectives/Targets	Activities/Strategies	Assessment/IEP/Evaluation
P4 *cont.*	Shows interest in continuing to explore tactile media in a range of ways. Asks for 'more/again' in some way. Makes marks on paper with hands and large pens, brushes, etc.	Use of wide range of tools to make marks with including sand tray, dough, paints, etc.	
P5	Joins in with making recognisable circles and lines on paper with fingers and large brush/pen, etc. Begins to trace or overwrite own name.	As above increasing the practical aspects of pencil control to enable recognisable letter shape for own name, or opportunity to make own letter using ICT.	
P6	Shows understanding that certain sounds represent certain objects or letters, e.g own letter represents their own name. Attempts to write own letter name independently as they hear sound.	Activities such as matching letters to pictures, linking objects to letters, e.g. collect all those beginning with this letter. Finding certain letters in stories and rhymes as they hear them.	
P7	Joins in with identifying letter sounds of other pupils in the class and attempts to write them down. Recognises many of them in written form. Joins in with writing down letters linked to familiar objects.	Emergent writing of own name and other letters in response to sounds and words they want to write about. Adult support to talk through their own news.	
P8	In response to sound of own letter and those of other pupils is able to write the correct and recognisable letter shape. Begins to write wider range of letters in response to sounds.		

Suggested books, other resources
Clicker with appropriate ready made or self made grid: Crick.
Letter Cluster books: *Alphabet starter.* Pub: Folens.
Range of tactile resources, e.g. sand tray, light pen, paint. Own name cards/symbols. Class words and class books.
Collection of objects from 2.2.

WORD LEVEL: PHONOLOGICAL AWARENESS, PHONICS AND SPELLING

W.L. YR: LO 2.4

Knowledge of grapheme/phoneme correspondences through identifying and writing initial and dominant phonemes in spoken words.

See also: W.L. YR: LO 2.1, 2.3, 2.5; W.L. Yr 1 Term 1: LO 3, 6

Steps	Learning Objectives/Targets	Activities/Strategies	Assessment/IEP/Evaluation
P1	i) Encounters and experiences a range of tactile objects with constant adult intervention naming each in turn, encouraging tactile exploration to establish object awareness and constancy. ii) Shows awareness of objects and focuses attention on some objects attending briefly to adult naming.	Sensory stimulation programmes based on tactile awareness such as hand massages, tactile media, etc. Adult provides opportunities for pupils to handle/look at objects and identifies object, stressing initial sound.	
P2	i) Responds to objects by looking and/or feeling and by actively exploring them. ii) Shows preference for certain objects and cooperates as adult names the objects as they interact.	As above using increasing range of objects and activities to promote tactile awareness, e.g. using pasta, jelly, rice, small bricks, sand water to encourage 'searching' and hand movements.	
P3	i) Points to certain objects that he/she wishes to explore. Sustains concentration for short period as adult explains the name, and initial sound/phoneme. ii) Anticipates missing objects, and looks for hidden object as adult names.	As above with increased opportunities for pupils to explore, anticipate, search and find objects in a range of different settings.	
P4	Shows interest in new objects and begins to 'give me' and name identified familiar object. Tries to 'draw' objects/people, etc., by scribble pictures as adult names them.	Whole class or individual games in which adult requests toy and pupils identify or give on request, e.g. 'Give me the dog' or 'Where's teddy'. Opportunities to make marks on paper, e.g. draw dog.	
P5	Joins in with naming/signing new and wider range of objects and pictures of objects. Traces and overwrites simple words as adult emphases sounds and phonemes as appropriate.	Teacher uses whole class discussion and group work with range of objects and books to increase pupils' language and knowledge of names of objects. Object/picture matching games. Collections of similar objects, e.g. a table full of teddy bears/cars/trains/books, etc.	

Suggested books, other resources
First Keys Alphabet to Literacy: Widgit.
Alphabats. Pub: Ginn.
* *I Blew a Bubble* by Bev Kemp. Pub: Learning Media, Ltd item 96/12.
Collections of objects beginning with relevant letter/sound.
Range of tactile resources, e.g. sand tray, light pen, paint. Sound LOTTO and Sound Tapes, e.g. LDA.

WORD LEVEL: PHONOLOGICAL AWARENESS, PHONICS AND SPELLING

W.L. YR: LO 2.4 cont.

Knowledge of grapheme/phoneme correspondences through identifying and writing initial and dominant phonemes in spoken words.

See also: W.L. YR: LO 2.1, 2.3, 2.5; W.L. Yr 1 Term 1: LO 3, 6

Steps	Learning Objectives/Targets	Activities/Strategies	Assessment/IEP/Evaluation
P6	Shows understanding that some objects begin with the same sound, and that they can be represented by a letter shape. Begins to draw recognisable objects and people and with support writes words. Begins to identify dominant sounds/phonemes and attempts to write them.	Collections of objects as P5, with adult modelling initial letters as pupils identify, e.g. 'What this? . . . A car . . . What does car begin with . . . c.c.c . . . it looks like this' (adult models 'C' on the board). Teacher uses small groups and 1:1 to stress initial and dominant sounds in words and where possible pupils copy as adult models, e.g. they make a 'C' in the air, on their board, or point to one on an answer board.	
P7	Joins in with identifying initial and dominant sounds/phonemes of wider range of objects and attempts to write them down or indicate on an answer board or keyboard. Some letters are correctly formed.	Using pictures of objects, and pictures from different texts, adult encourages pupils to identify initial sounds and attempt to write/indicate each. Matching games with pictures and letters, e.g. put all the things beginning with 'P' in this circle. Listening games, e.g. 'what sound does pig/pin, pat/put begin with? Show me what "p" looks like.'	
P8	Identifies dominant phonemes in familiar words and can write them down or indicate them on an answer board or keyboard.	As P7 using pictures of objects with dominant phonemes as well as initial ones so that pupils are encouraged to listen carefully and indicate correct phoneme as adult stresses it, e.g. 'can you tell me what sounds you can hear in "shell"/"shut"/"ship"', etc.	

Suggested books, other resources
First Keys Alphabet to Literacy: Widgit.
Alphabats. Pub: Ginn.
* *I Blew a Bubble* by Bev Kemp. Pub: Learning Media, Ltd item 96/12.
Collections of objects beginning with relevant letter/sound.
Range of tactile resources, e.g. sand tray, light pen, paint. Sound LOTTO and Sound Tapes, e.g. LDA.

WORD LEVEL: PHONOLOGICAL AWARENESS, PHONICS AND SPELLING

W.L. YR: LO 2.5

Knowledge of grapheme/phoneme correspondences through identifying and writing initial and final phonemes in consonant–vowel–consonant (CVC).

See also: W.L. YR: LO 2.1, 2.3, 2.4; W.L. Yr 1 Term 1: LO 6

Steps	Learning Objectives/Targets	Activities/Strategies	Assessment/IEP/Evaluation
P1	i) Encounters and experiences a range of sensory activities to encourage listening skills. ii) Shows emerging awareness of sounds and reacts to different levels of sound and range of spoken sounds.	Listening programmes, using musical instruments, stopping and starting, singing rhymes, whole class stories in which adult emphasises word endings, using the same endings to ensure understanding, e.g. 'I'll huff and I'll puff'. Noisy toys, e.g. squeaky bears, bells, etc.	
P2	i) Responds consistently to listening activities and shows interest by body movement or vocalisation as adult initiates noises and activities. ii) Vocalises and gestures in response to certain musical and spoken sounds.	As P1 with adult stressing initial and final sounds in words continuously. Stories such as, The Three Little Pigs, The Three Billy Goats Gruff, Humpty Dumpty.	
P3	i) Participates in shared activities by vocalising, joining in at appropriate time with musical or story type activities. ii) Anticipates sounds during listening activities, by moving head/face/body or by 'searching' for the sound in some way.	Whole class, small group and individual work to provide many opportunities for pupils to hear sounds, wait for a particular sound, identify different sounds, e.g. sound lotto games with adult encouraging anticipation be saying 'what's next . . . listen . . . here it comes . . .'. Stories as P2 to enable pupils to anticipate familiar endings. Listening to instruments behind a screen and trying to indicate which one it was.	
P4	Shows interest in an increasing range of listening activities such as the dinner trolley/certain familiar voices/familiar classroom sounds/toys that make a noise. Repeats and copies sounds as adult makes them.	Opportunities for pupils to make sounds of their own. Copying adult sounds. Clapping names. Adult shows object and begins to name 'Look it's a ca . . . t' stressing final sounds. Encourage copying, e.g. 'Now you, . . . it's a ca . . .'.	

Suggested books, other resources
Clicker with appropriate ready made or self made grid: Crick.
The Three Little Pigs – retold by Brenda Parkes & Judith Smith. Pub: Rigby. ISBN 07312 1043 (large) 07327 0539 (small).
Class list of objects/photographs/pictures/symbols/words of the same endings. Sound letters, tape recorders. Listening games, e.g. LDA.

WORD LEVEL: PHONOLOGICAL AWARENESS, PHONICS AND SPELLING

W.L. YR: LO 2.5 *cont.*

Knowledge of grapheme/phoneme correspondences through identifying and writing initial and final phonemes in consonant–vowel–consonant (CVC).

See also: W.L. YR: LO 2.1, 2.3, 2.4; W.L. Yr 1 Term 1: LO 6

Steps	Learning Objectives/Targets	Activities/Strategies	Assessment/IEP/Evaluation
P5	Joins in with naming recognisable toys based on CVC words, e.g. cat/dog/bat. Names familiar, people and objects, and joins in with aspects of familiar stories.	Adult uses a range of rhyming stories to stress initial and final sounds. Pupils listen and repeat.	
P6	Shows understanding that objects and toys are represented by letters, and begins to recognise initial letters of some words, particularly those that begin with the same initial letter as their own.	In small groups or 1:1 pupils listen again to rhyming stories as adult stresses initial sounds and shows how they are written down. Pupils attempt to copy initial letters.	
P7	Joins in with identifying initial and some final sounds in familiar words.	As P6, with adult stressing initial and final sounds in words. Pupils copy or indicate.	
P8	Identifies initial and final sounds in familiar CVC words and attempts to write them down.	Wide range of activities based on CVC words, e.g. word and picture matching. Pictures to match the initial sounds to, and then the final sounds.	

Suggested books, other resources

Clicker with appropriate ready made or self made grid: Crick.
The Three Little Pigs – retold by Brenda Parkes & Judith Smith. Pub: Rigby. ISBN 07312 1043 (large) 07327 0539 (small).
Class list of objects/photographs/pictures/symbols/words of the same endings. Sound letters, tape recorders. Listening games, e.g. LDA.

WORD LEVEL: PHONOLOGICAL AWARENESS, PHONICS AND SPELLING

W.L. YR: LO 3.1

Alphabetical and phonic knowledge through sounding and naming each letter of the alphabet in lower and upper case.

See also: W.L. YR: LO 3.2, 3.3; W.L. Yr 1 Term 1: LO 2

Steps	Learning Objectives/Targets	Activities/Strategies	Assessment/IEP/Evaluation
P1	i) Encounters and experiences a range of multi-sensory activities to promote looking and listening skills, and regularly hears own name. ii) Shows awareness of activities in which own name is sung/said, and in which familiar objects are named.	Use of multi-sensory rooms and equipment to develop visual and auditory awareness, e.g. looking and following lights, auditory feedback games, listening to music, etc. Singing rhymes.	
P2	i) Responds consistently to multi-sensory input such as by turning head towards lights, following or tracking a moving light or object, and by responding to hearing own name called or object named. ii) Recognises familiar objects and shows pleasure when certain ones appear. Tries to imitate adult naming of objects.	As for P1 and use of daily routines, name cards, activities involving names, such as singing Hello songs emphasising each name and its initial sound.	
P3	i) Participates in shared activities in which familiar objects, toys, people are named with emphasis on initial sounds. ii) Anticipates own name during class sessions, and starts to look for the 'next thing' during multi-sensory activities.	As P1 and P2, plus encouraging anticipation by saying 'who's next' or 'wait for it . . . here it comes'. Begin use of name/symbol/photograph cards for names, e.g. holding the card adult says 'where's John?' Pupil is encouraged through praise to respond in some way and to anticipate what's coming next, e.g. 'Who else begins with J'.	
P4	Shows interest in names of other pupils in the class and looks towards them when their name is called. Shows interest in own familiar objects and looks towards them. Finds objects 'the same'.	To encourage interest adult uses alphabet songs and rhymes with letter/picture/photograph matching activities when trying to encourage pupils to recognise own name card and familiar objects and people, e.g. own coat, cup, chair, mum, dad, etc., emphasising the sound of each initial letter.	

Suggested books, other resources

Talking Animated Alphabet: Sherston.
Teddy Bear Alphabet by Pamela Slack. Pub: Shortlands Publications Ltd. ISBN 0-7901-1539-5.
* *The Absolutely Brilliant Crazy Party* by Wendy Body; Pelican Big Book. Pub: Longman. ISBN 0582 333466 (large) 0582 33747X (small).
Set of upper and lower case letter cards with pictures of objects beginning with relevant letter. Own name/symbol cards.
'Own' objects. Name/symbol cards of other pupils/objects.

WORD LEVEL: PHONOLOGICAL AWARENESS, PHONICS AND SPELLING

W.L. YR: LO 3.1 *cont.*

Alphabetical and phonic knowledge through sounding and naming each letter of the alphabet in lower and upper case.

See also: W.L. YR: LO 3.2, 3.3; W.L. Yr 1 Term 1: LO 2

Steps	Learning Objectives/Targets	Activities/Strategies	Assessment/IEP/Evaluation
P5	Recognises pictures of familiar people and objects and begins to name them or find a symbol to represent them. Attempts to say initial sound of own name.	Adult continues to use alphabet songs and rhymes with pupils joining in. In small groups or individually, encourages recognition and naming of pictures and symbols.	
P6	Recognises own capital letter. Shows understanding that names are different and that each has its own letter. Reads up to 10 familiar letters and matches initial letters.	Continue activities as above, also whole class name games using upper case letters to match pupils' names, e.g. 'Whose name begins with J?' and 'Let's find some more things that begin with J' and 'Let's read this rhyme together and see if we can find the letter J' (Jack and Jill, Jack Sprat).	
P7	Joins in with identifying the initial sounds and letters of other pupils' names. Understands that objects have names and that they begin with certain letters. Recognises some upper and some lower case letters, and names them or finds them on an answer board.	As above as well as matching activities using upper and lower case with pictures/photographs. In small groups or individually, pupils use books, names and labels to see the difference between upper and lower case. Use of alphabet books and friezes to foster further understanding.	
P8	Joins in with singing or saying/signing the alphabet, and recognises an increasing number of upper and lower case letters.	As above with increased activities to improve phonic and alphabetical knowledge by linking activities, e.g. collections of objects beginning with certain sounds so that pupils can say the sound and name the letter.	

Suggested books, other resources
Talking Animated Alphabet: Sherston.
Teddy Bear Alphabet by Pamela Slack. Pub: Shortlands Publications Ltd. ISBN 0-7901-1539-5.
* *The Absolutely Brilliant Crazy Party* by Wendy Body; Pelican Big Book. Pub: Longman. ISBN 0582 333466 (large) 0582 33747X (small).
Set of upper and lower case letter cards with pictures of objects beginning with relevant letter. Own name/symbol cards.
'Own' objects. Name/symbol cards of other pupils/objects.

WORD LEVEL: PHONOLOGICAL AWARENESS, PHONICS AND SPELLING

W.L. YR: LO 3.2

Alphabetical and phonic knowledge through writing letters in response to letter names.

See also: W.L. YR: LO 3.1, 8, 12, 13, 14; S.L. YR: LO 4; T.L. YR: LO 11.4, 11.5, 12.2

Steps	Learning Objectives/Targets	Activities/Strategies	Assessment/IEP/Evaluation
P1	i) Encounters and experiences a range of multi-sensory activities to encourage tactile awareness. ii) Shows an emerging awareness of different textures and begins to focus on hands.	Use of multi-sensory rooms to promote touching, holding, feeling different media and to encourage enjoyment in the feel of different objects. Use differing textures and temperatures to stimulate awareness (link to 3.1 and 2.3). Hand massages and link to physiotherapy hand function programmes.	
P2	i) Responds to the different tactile experiences by body movement or vocalisation, or by beginning to move fingers. ii) Actively explores different media and focuses attention on sensory exploration.	As above with increasing encouragement and praise as pupil begins to move hands and fingers. Multi-sensory approaches, guides pupils to 'look' or 'feel' as well as listen during activities.	
P3	i) Actively looks for objects hidden in sand, water, etc. Reaches out for familiar and favourite objects as adult names them. ii) Begins to apply solutions by searching in different ways for objects and items they require. Anticipates finding named objects by showing excitement.	In 1:1 adult uses range of multi-sensory approaches to develop fine motor skills.	
P4	Shows interest in finding certain items hidden in different media. Searches for given item such as a 'ball'. Repeats and copies adult naming. Scribbles, explores paint with hands.	As above with increasing number of different objects to increase the amount of hand function, and mobility that each pupil has. Where hand function is limited pupil may need to indicate objects by looking or eye-pointing. Use of sand/water/dough, etc. to encourage movement.	

Suggested books, other resources

Clicker with appropriate ready made or self made grid: Crick.
Own name/symbols/photograph cards.
Paper/board/tactile material, e.g. clay, dough, sand tray, light pen. Class rota, timetables, job labels.
Letter books and collections of tactile objects beginning with the same letter.

WORD LEVEL: PHONOLOGICAL AWARENESS, PHONICS AND SPELLING

W.L. YR: LO 3.2 *cont.*

Alphabetical and phonic knowledge through writing letters in response to letter names.

See also: W.L. YR: LO 3.1, 8, 12, 13, 14; S.L. YR: LO 4; T.L. YR: LO 11.4, 11.5, 12.2

Steps	Learning Objectives/Targets	Activities/Strategies	Assessment/IEP/Evaluation
P5	Begins to make marks on paper with brushes, light pens, pens, etc. Names objects on request and attempts to draw them or scribble write. Copies over adult writing.	Range of drawing, painting activities as well as increased object recognition games.	
P6	Recognises own picture/symbol/name and attempts to make the shape of own initial letter in sand/paint/pencil, etc. Understands that objects have names and that they have different initial sounds Copies other letters.	Copy initial letter of own name in as many ways as possible, and encourage recognition and writing of initial letters of other pupils' names and objects where possible. Make use of multi-sensory approach, sand tray, light pen, IT.	
P7	Joins in with attempting to write down many different letters as adult requests.	In small groups or whole class, pupils write letters for 'letter books', make collections of same letter objects. Read alphabet using words or signs.	
P8	Becomes increasingly independent in writing/forming a wider range of letters in response to letter names.	As above with increasing opportunities to write independently and begin emergent writing. Pupils use tactile 3D representation to 'collect' more letters.	

Suggested books, other resources
Clicker with appropriate ready made or self made grid: Crick.
Own name/symbols/photograph cards.
Paper/board/tactile material, e.g. clay, dough, sand tray, light pen. Class rota, timetables, job labels.
Letter books and collections of tactile objects beginning with the same letter.

WORD LEVEL: PHONOLOGICAL AWARENESS, PHONICS AND SPELLING

W.L. YR: LO 3.3

Alphabetical and phonic knowledge through understanding alphabetical order through alphabet books, rhymes and songs.

See also: W.L. YR 1 Term 1: LO 2

Steps	Learning Objectives/Targets	Activities/Strategies	Assessment/IEP/Evaluation
P1	i) Encounters and experiences adult voices singing and saying different rhymes and songs including alphabet songs. ii) Shows some awareness of adult voices and presence and begins to focus on sound of voice singing and talking.	Adults sing range of songs, nursery rhymes, etc., makes animal sounds, transport noises, etc.	
P2	i) Shows awareness and interest in sound of adult voice singing or saying rhymes, including alphabet rhymes. Focuses attention on adult face and responds in some way to adult voices and noises. ii) Vocalises and gestures, e.g. turns head towards adult voice. Shows pleasure in listening to familiar rhymes.	As P1. Adult also signs/reads alphabet songs/stories/rhymes using picture books to reinforce alphabetical order.	
P3	i) Seeks to join in with familiar rhymes and songs, vocalises in time to music or rhythm. ii) Anticipates sounds and noises made by adults and others by turning towards or by body and eye movements, e.g. vocalising, gesture.	Teacher/adult uses and re-uses songs, noises including alphabet songs and rhymes.	
P4	Copies and imitates adult voice as they listen to and join in with alphabetical songs and stories and rhymes. Shows interest in songs and rhymes linked to certain sounds.	Teacher/adult with whole class or group encourages pupils to join in rhymes and songs.	

Suggested books, other resources
Clicker with appropriate ready made or self made grid: Crick
Teddy Bear Alphabet by Paula Slack. Pub: Shortlands Publications Ltd. ISBN 0-7901-1539-5.
Sing the Alphabet Fruits and Veg from A–Z by Lois Ehlert (ed.). Harcourt Brace & Company. ISBN 0-15-2009-02-7.
Class alphabet songs. Letter/picture cards.

WORD LEVEL: PHONOLOGICAL AWARENESS, PHONICS AND SPELLING

W.L. YR: LO 3.3 *cont.*

Alphabetical and phonic knowledge through understanding alphabetical order through alphabet books, rhymes and songs.

See also: W.L. YR 1 Term 1: LO 2

Steps	Learning Objectives/Targets	Activities/Strategies	Assessment/IEP/Evaluation
P5	Begins to make sounds linked to activities such as animal noises, transport noises, and some alphabetical sounds, e.g. da.da.da. Follows requests to find certain objects beginning with a letter or sound.	Through songs and rhymes in whole class and small groups pupils begin to make sounds at appropriate times. Join in with sounds during stories, e.g. 'What did the duck say'? Quack Quack.	
P6	Recognises and copies sounds made by adults and pupils, e.g. 'What does cat begin with' . . . c.c.c and links it to the letter name.	Range of activities based on alphabet sounds, books and songs to encourage understanding of alphabetical knowledge and order.	
P7	Matches letters of the alphabet and begins to say some sequences, e.g. ABCD . . . XYZ.		
P8	Joins in with singing some alphabetical letter names in order. Says or sings at least part of the alphabet. Recognises the order of some of the alphabetical letters.	Repetitive singing and saying of the alphabet. Regular use of alphabet books. Collections of pictures and objects linked to certain letter sounds. Making own alphabet books. As above with continuous repetition and alphabetical activities.	

Suggested books, other resources
Clicker with appropriate ready made or self made grid: Crick
Teddy Bear Alphabet by Paula Slack. Pub: Shortlands Publications Ltd. ISBN 0-7901-1539-5.
Sing the Alphabet Fruits and Veg from A–Z by Lois Ehlert (ed.). Harcourt Brace & Company. ISBN 0-15-2009-02-7.
Class alphabet songs. Letter/picture cards.

WORD LEVEL: PHONOLOGICAL AWARENESS, PHONICS AND SPELLING

W.L. YR: LO 4.1

To link sound and spelling patterns by using knowledge of rhyme to identify families of rhyming CVC words.

See also: W.L. YR: LO 1.1; W.L. Yr 1 Term 1: LO 3, 5

Steps	Learning Objectives/Targets	Activities/Strategies	Assessment/IEP/Evaluation
P1	As LO 1.1. i) Encounters and experiences rhyming songs and poems as part of a group on a regular basis. ii) Shows emerging awareness of adult voice reading or singing familiar rhymes and families of rhyming words.	Adult reads/recites a range of simple rhymes/songs/poems until they become increasingly familiar. Singing and saying families of rhyming words to ensure familiarity with sounds.	
P2	i) Responds to continuous experience of hearing familiar rhyming songs and poems by vocalising or body movement. ii) Interacts with adult by communicating in some way their preferences or enjoyment as they listen to rhymes and groups of rhyming words.	Adult creates opportunities for pupils to hear familiar songs and rhymes on a daily basis using encouraging sounds to help pupil respond.	
P3	i) Tries to join in with familiar repetitive rhymes or groups of rhyming words by body movement vocalisations or eye contact. ii) Anticipates the endings of rhymes and songs as adult sings/says and then hesitates.	Adult sings and says range of familiar songs and rhymes, pausing at the appropriate time. Use listening, singing, action games and objects. Offer choices.	
P4	Shows interest in activities relating to rhyme, such as choosing a rhyming song, or vocalising as rhyme takes place. Imitates adult voice.	Opportunities for pupils to imitate and copy sequences of rhyming words, e.g. hat, cat, sat, mat, etc.	

Suggested books, other resources
Rhyme and analogy activity software: Sherston.
Finger Fun and Action Rhymes by Wendy Body; Pelican Big Books. Pub: Longman. ISBN 0582 33344X (large) 0582 333539 (small).
* *City Rhymes* by Judy Naylor. Pub: Modern Curriculum Publishers. ISBN 0-8136-1106-7.

WORD LEVEL: PHONOLOGICAL AWARENESS, PHONICS AND SPELLING

W.L. YR: LO 4.1 *cont.*

To link sound and spelling patterns by using knowledge of rhyme to identify families of rhyming CVC words.

See also: W.L. YR: LO 1.1; W.L. Yr 1 Term 1: LO 3, 5

Steps	Learning Objectives/Targets	Activities/Strategies	Assessment/IEP/Evaluation
P5	Follows request to add to one or two CVC rhyming words. Follows simple story or rhyme which includes families of rhyming words. Matches pictures of words that rhyme.	Teacher reads and re-reads or sings familiar rhymes, encouraging pupils to join in/feel the rhythm/indicate symbols to show that they are following the rhyme.	
P6	Recognises some rhyming words in familiar simple texts.	In small groups or individually pupils indicate which words rhyme in familiar rhymes and songs.	
P7	Joins in with finding words that rhyme in a familiar poem or song, e.g. Humpty Dumpty. Predicts which rhyming word comes next in a simple rhyme or story.	Using a flip chart with clearly printed words/symbols/pictures, adult writes simple rhyme so that pupils can see and join in with finding 'words that sound the same'.	
P8	Recognises rhyme in less familiar songs and rhymes, as well as in stories.	As P7 using a wider range of rhyming words, songs and stories.	

Suggested books, other resources
Rhyme and analogy activity software: Sherston.
Finger Fun and Action Rhymes by Wendy Body; Pelican Big Books. Pub: Longman. ISBN 0582 33344X (large) 0582 333539 (small).
* *City Rhymes* by Judy Naylor. Pub: Modern Curriculum Publishers. ISBN 0-8136-1106-7.

WORD LEVEL: PHONOLOGICAL AWARENESS, PHONICS AND SPELLING

W.L. YR: LO 4.2

To link sound and spelling patterns by identifying discriminating 'onsets' from 'rhymes' in speech and spelling.

See also: W.L. YR: LO 4.1

Steps	Learning Objectives/Targets	Activities/Strategies	Assessment/IEP/Evaluation
P8	Following on from 4.1. Recognises that rhyming words have different initial letter(s).	Following 4.1 pupil undertakes matching activities with words, pictures and symbols to change initial letter(s) in rhyming words in songs and simple rhymes, e.g. <u>c</u>at, <u>mat</u>.	

Suggested books, other resources
Nursery Rhyme Time: Sherston.
Nursery Rhymes. Pub: Ginn.
ABC and Rhyme book. Pub: Ginn.
* *Rat-a-Tat-Tat* by Jill Eggleton. Pub: Kingscourt.
Cards/symbols of initial letters/final graphemes. Lists of rhyming words, rhyming sentences.

WORD LEVEL: PHONOLOGICAL AWARENESS, PHONICS AND SPELLING

W.L. YR: LO 4.3

To link sound and spelling patterns by identifying alliteration in known, new and invented words.

See also: W.L. YR: LO 1.2; T.L. Yr 1 Term 1: LO 6

Steps	Learning Objectives/Targets	Activities/Strategies	Assessment/IEP/Evaluation
P1	i) Encounters and experiences range of poems, rhymes and stories with alliterative content. ii) Begins to show awareness of adult voice and activities as rhymes and stories take place.	Teacher reads appropriate stories, stressing alliteration passages and repeating them to ensure they become familiar.	
P2	i) Responds through body movement to hearing stories and rhymes that include simple alliteration. ii) Shows pleasure and interest by trying to join in or communicate as activities take place.	As P1 with increasing opportunities to show a response by body or eye movements.	
P3	i) Begins to participate in simple activities which stimulate involvement through gesture or vocalisation. ii) Anticipates parts of stories that include alliteration, e.g. 'Billy Goats Gruff' . . . trip trap trip trap, etc. by body/eye movements.	In groups or whole class pupils are involved in a range of listening games, and activities in which they hear stories and rhymes with alliteration so that they can begin to anticipate the next word.	
P4	Shows interest in stories and rhymes with alliteration and attempts to vocalise as they copy and imitate parts of the story.	In small groups and individually, pupils hear different combinations of sounds as adults create alliteration, encouraging them to join in.	
P5	Begins to respond to simple questioning about alliteration and gives simple examples by completing a phrase.	Adult uses familiar stories such as those mentioned encouraging pupils to complete the alliteration, stressing the initial sounds.	

Suggested books, other resources
First Keys To Literacy: Widgit.
Peter Piper, Illus. Susan Swan. Pub: Ginn. ISBN 0-602-28032-A.
See also *Jumbled, Tumbled Tales and Rhymes.* Pub: Ginn.
Splishes & Sploshes, selected by Debbie Powell and Andrea Butler. Pub: Globe Press. ISBN 0947 328 64X.
Collections and objects/pictures with same initial letter. Listening games, e.g. LDA.

WORD LEVEL: PHONOLOGICAL AWARENESS, PHONICS AND SPELLING

W.L. YR: LO 4.3 cont.

To link sound and spelling patterns by identifying alliteration in known, new and invented words.

See also: W.L. YR: LO 1.2; T.L. Yr 1 Term 1: LO 6

Steps	Learning Objectives/Targets	Activities/Strategies	Assessment/IEP/Evaluation
P6	Re-tell parts of simple stories that include alliteration, e.g. Rumpelstiltskin 'Fee Fie Fo Fum', etc.	Activities in which pupils vocalise nonsense words using a familiar initial letter . . . perhaps their own. Adult uses different strategies to help foster understanding of alliteration, e.g. explore objects and describe them as 'blue ball' 'Big blue ball', etc.	
P7	Begins to predict and suggest alliterative words within sentences, including nonsense words.	As P6. Continue to describe objects and say rhymes to help consolidate understanding.	
P8	Joins in with making nonsense alliteration. Identifies simple alliteration in simple familiar stories.	Adult uses flip chart/symbols/voice and pictures to encourage pupils to use alliteration and find it in rhymes and stories.	

Suggested books, other resources
First Keys To Literacy: Widgit.
Peter Piper, Illus. Susan Swan. Pub: Ginn. ISBN 0-602-28032-A.
See also *Jumbled, Tumbled Tales and Rhymes.* Pub: Ginn.
Splishes & Sploshes, selected by Debbie Powell and Andrea Butler. Pub: Globe Press. ISBN 0947 328 64X.
Collections and objects/pictures with same initial letter. Listening games, e.g. LDA.

WORD LEVEL: WORD RECOGNITION, GRAPHIC KNOWLEDGE AND SPELLING

W.L. YR: LO 5

To read on sight a range of familiar words, e.g. children's names, captions, labels and words from favourite books.

See also: W.L. YR: LO 6, 7; T.L. YR: LO 8; W.L. Yr 1 Term 1: LO 7, 8, 9; T.L. Yr 1 Term 1: LO 12, 13

Steps	Learning Objectives/Targets	Activities/Strategies	Assessment/IEP/Evaluation
P1	i) Encounters and experiences being part of a group in which they hear names daily, and in which they regularly hear names of familiar objects. ii) Shows an emerging awareness of own name when it is called. Begins to focus on objects.	Daily activities to encourage pupils to recognise own belongings, e.g. 'Whose coat is this?' 'Whose name is this?'. Register symbols/names. Daily routines.	
P2	i) Responds in some way to hearing own name, or to seeing own symbol. Responds to everyday objects, e.g. cup, biscuit by body/eye movements. ii) Tries to make a response when name is called through vocalising or gesturing. Understands that all pupils have a name and answer in turn.	Use a range of everyday objects in whole class situations/ group or 1:1 to elicit recognition. Constant use of pupils' names.	
P3	i) Communicates intentionally as they participate in registration and other activities in which they recognise the sound of own name, objects and people, and in which symbols and word cards are used ii) Anticipates what comes next in registration times, lunch times, and home time. Looks towards own objects when named.	Use a range of everyday familiar objects. Encourage anticipation by saying 'who's next?' in registration.	

Suggested books, other resources
Clicker with appropriate ready made or self made grid: Crick.
Anna's Amazing Multi-Coloured Glasses by Wendy Body; Pelican Big Book. Pub: Longman. ISBN 0582 333482 (large) 0582 337437 (small).
Own labelled belongings. Own names/symbols.
Appropriate language programme, e.g. Derbyshire Language Scheme.
Collections of objects or photographs of self and family members.

WORD LEVEL: WORD RECOGNITION, GRAPHIC KNOWLEDGE AND SPELLING

W. L. YR: LO 5 *cont.*

To read on sight a range of familiar words, e.g. children's names, captions, labels and words from favourite books.

See also: W.L. YR: LO 6, 7; T.L. YR: LO 8; W.L. Yr 1 Term 1: LO 7, 8, 9; T.L. Yr 1 Term 1: LO 12, 13

Steps	Learning Objectives/Targets	Activities/Strategies	Assessment/IEP/Evaluation
P4	Shows interest in finding own familiar objects. Makes choices of own coat, cup, symbol, picture, and shows recognition by vocalising or body movement.	Use of pupils' own objects, names, name symbols and cards in groups, labels in classroom, daily tasks, classroom objects.	
P5	Begins to recognise simple pictures in a picture or photograph book, and names them/signs.	Make own books of familiar objects or pupils family. Make simple captions.	
P6	Recognises photos/pictures/symbols/word card of self and familiar peers. Recognises photos of own familiar objects, matches words and letters. Finds familiar words around the classroom and in books.	In 1:1, add one word caption to pictures or photographs, e.g. mummy, car, dog.	
P7	Joins in with reading simple name cards of all the pupils in the class. Reads some labels in the classroom with words or symbols.	Pupils take it in turns to read/sign name cards at beginning of day.	
P8	Reads names, labels and simple captions in own photo book. Reads a growing number of familiar words or symbols.	Pupils make own books (with support) so that they can make a simple photograph book with one word captions that they learn to read.	

Suggested books, other resources
Clicker with appropriate ready made or self made grid: Crick.
Anna's Amazing Multi-Coloured Glasses by Wendy Body; Pelican Big Book. Pub: Longman. ISBN 0582 333482 (large) 0582 337437 (small).
Own labelled belongings. Own names/symbols.
Appropriate language programme, e.g. Derbyshire Language Scheme.
Collections of objects or photographs of self and family members.

WORD LEVEL: WORD RECOGNITION, GRAPHIC KNOWLEDGE AND SPELLING

W.L. YR: LO 6

To read on sight the 45 high frequency words to be taught by the end of reception year from favourite books.

See also: W.L. YR: LO 5, 7; W.L. Yr 1 Term 1: LO 7, 8, 9 W.L. YR: LO 6, 7; T.L. YR: LO 7, 8, 9; W.L. Yr 1 Term 1: LO 7, 8, 9; T.L. Yr 1 Term 1: LO 12, 13

Steps	Learning Objectives/Targets	Activities/Strategies	Assessment/IEP/Evaluation
P7	From LO 5. Recognises own name and own labels from belongings, labels round classroom. As W.L. YR: LO 5.	In whole class, group or individual work using games relating to own names, letter sounds, words and symbols around the classroom. Whole word recognition to be linked to class stories.	
P8	Reads/signs familiar words in own photograph book and then some around the classroom and gradually adds some of the 45 high frequency words each week.	Continual repetition and use of words, pictures and symbols to develop social sight vocabulary/signing. Ensure that the high frequency words introduced are accompanied by multi-sensory resources to ensure learning takes place, e.g. tactile, visually clear word cards and simple caption books.	

Suggested books, other resources
Talking Write Away: Black Cat.
Photograph books of self and family.
* Topic books using photographs and pictures with appropriate words.
Own name cards/photographs/symbols. High frequency words on cards. Social vocabulary/symbols on cards.

WORD LEVEL: WORD RECOGNITION, GRAPHIC KNOWLEDGE AND SPELLING

W.L. YR: LO 7

To read on sight the words from texts of appropriate difficulty.

See also: W.L. YR: LO 5, 6; W.L. Yr 1 Term 1: LO 9

Steps	Learning Objectives/Targets	Activities/Strategies	Assessment/IEP/Evaluation
P6	Recognises photographs or pictures relating to self and family by indicating, smiling.	Individually or in groups use matching to relate self/family to photographs. With adult create own photograph 'life' with 1 and 2 word captions written by adult.	
P7	Joins in with reading familiar words such as names, captions and labels. Recognises that print in books has meaning and reads some simple words in text. Shows understanding of the conventions of reading. Follows left to right.	Teacher uses familiar big book or own book. Asks pupils to speak, vocalise or sign words matched to pictures. These recorded on flip chart. Make own book using familiar words and matching to pictures.	
P8	Reads familiar words in simple text increasing the range and number.	1:1, pupil reads simple sight vocabulary from topic books and simple reading books.	

Suggested books, other resources
Clicker with appropriate ready made or self made grid: Crick.
Photograph books of self and family.
* Topic books using photographs and pictures with appropriate words.
Appropriate reading scheme.
Word cards/symbols/pictures. Lists of words to make different captions.

WORD LEVEL: WORD RECOGNITION, GRAPHIC KNOWLEDGE AND SPELLING

W.L. YR: LO 8

To read and write own name and explore other words related to the spelling of own name.

See also: W.L. YR: LO 2.2, 3.2, 5; W.L. Yr 1 Term 1: LO 8

Steps	Learning Objectives/Targets	Activities/Strategies	Assessment/IEP/Evaluation
P7	From LO 2.2, 3.2 and 5. Reads own name on familiar name card and writes own name given model to copy. Writes own initial letter correctly or indicates it on a keyboard as T.L. YR: LO 12.2. Many letters are formed correctly.	Use of daily routine activities, e.g. registration, dinner choices, jobs, timetables to raise awareness of own name. Own familiar name card to read and copy.	
P8	Reads own name in different situations, and recognises other words that begin with the same initial letter. Writes own name and recognises that of others T.L. YR: LO 11.4 and 11.5.	Individually or in small group use word lotto, matching own name/sign and photographs. Daily practice in writing own name in different contexts, and recognising own initial letter in other words.	

Suggested books, other resources
Clicker with appropriate ready made or self made grid: Crick
Own name cards/symbols.
Photograph books of self and family members.
Class word list.

WORD LEVEL: WORD RECOGNITION, GRAPHIC KNOWLEDGE AND SPELLING

W.L. YR: LO 9

To recognise the critical features of words, e.g. shape, length and common spelling patterns.

See also: W.L. Yr 1 Term 1: LO 10, 11

Steps	Learning Objectives/Targets	Activities/Strategies	Assessment/IEP/Evaluation
P6	Recognises own photo/symbol name card and knows that it is different to others. Recognise, up to 10 simple words linked to personal vocabulary.	During daily routines adult points out different name/symbol cards, giving opportunities for pupils to recognise own name.	
P7	Reads own name card and knows it is different to others. Shows awareness of the difference, such as 'longer', 'shorter', 'different'.	In 1:1 or small groups pupils compare own names/symbol card with that of others.	
P8	Recognises other words that begin with same initial sound, and comments on whether it is 'longer', 'shorter', etc. Recognises and reads simple and similar CVC words such as cat, mat, pat, etc. Recognises letters of the alphabet by shape.	Using unknown spelling patterns from rhymes and songs pupils match words to card shapes and discuss differences.	

Suggested books, other resources
First Keys to Literacy: Widget.
Class name card/symbol/photograph.
Lists of long/short words from familiar texts. Card shapes. Similar spellings lists.

WORD LEVEL: VOCABULARY EXTENSION

W.L. YR: LO 10

New words from their reading and shared experiences.

See also: W.L. YR: LO 11; W.L. Yr 1 Term 1: LO 12

Steps	Learning Objectives/Targets	Activities/Strategies	Assessment/IEP/Evaluation
P7	Recognises words in shared text and discussion that they have not 'met' before. Makes predictions about what the word might be, based on prior knowledge.	In whole class story time, pupils find new words linked to known initial sounds and spelling patterns and make lists for classroom display.	
P8	Identifies and reads simple new words. Joins in with using simple dictionaries to identify meanings of new words.	In whole class story time, pupils find new words and together work out how to read the word. Word is added to word list.	

Suggested books, other resources
My First Amazing Dictionary: Dorling Kindersley.
Looking at Teddy Bears by Sallie Purkis; Pelican Big Book. Pub: Longman. ISBN 0582 333 49 0 (large) 0582 333 58 X (small).
* *Long, Long Ago* by Judith McKinnon. Pub: Shorthand Publications. ISBN 0-790-0226-9.
* Simple home-made dictionaries.

WORD LEVEL: VOCABULARY EXTENSION

W.L. YR: LO 11

To make collections of personal interest or significant words and words linked to particular topics.

See also: W.L. YR: LO 10; W.L. Yr 1 Term 1: LO 12

Steps	Learning Objectives/Targets	Activities/Strategies	Assessment/IEP/Evaluation
P1	i) Encounters and experiences activities related to handling, seeing, own personal objects as adult names. ii) Shows awareness and begins to focus on own personal objects.	In small groups, whole class or 1:1, pupils 'collect' objects from a family holiday/visit or objects relating to personal interest.	
P2	i) Responds to own objects by smiling, reaching out to touch and exploring. ii) Begins to recognise own objects and shows pleasure at seeing or handling them.	Ensure objects belonging to pupils are placed around class where they can be seen.	
P3	i) Looks for own objects, points to them with hands or eyes. Plays with them and observes what happens. ii) Actively explores a range of objects for extended periods, plays with adult with different objects, takes turns.	To make individual books of own 'life' using photographs with 1 and 2 word captions. To make individual topic books with pictures and simple captions. To make whole class word/symbol books on a class topic, e.g. The weather.	
P4	Recognises familiar photos and begins to name own objects. Recognises them in picture form. Selects correct picture from a limited range on request. Talks about or signs own comments on pictures. Enjoys sharing pictures with adult words/signs/symbols connected to them.	Following the above activity in small groups, pupils read words and share photographs/pictures with others. As above, including range of single pictures for pupil to name and discuss.	

Suggested books, other resources
Clicker with appropriate ready made or self made grid: Crick
Photograph books of own life.
* Individual or class topic books.
* Unit A *Myself* topic books; Oxford Reading Trees. Pub: Oxford University Press.
See also other topic books in this series, e.g. *Houses and Homes*. Pub: Oxford University Press.

WORD LEVEL: VOCABULARY EXTENSION

W.L. YR: LO 11 *cont.*

To make collections of personal interest or significant words and words linked to particular topics.

See also: W.L. YR: LO 10; W.L. Yr 1 Term 1: LO 12

Steps	Learning Objectives/Targets	Activities/Strategies	Assessment/IEP/Evaluation
P6	Recognises and reads own name and some others, and begins to join in with reading words in own photo book, own topic collections and labels.	Pupils read together any whole class topic book which has simple sentences.	
P7	Reads simple sentences linked to own topic or personal pictures.	Increasing range of simple texts including own topic books.	
P8	Reads an increasing range of words associated with class and own topics.	In small groups or individually pupils make topic books which use a wider range of vocabulary.	

Suggested books, other resources
Clicker with appropriate ready made or self made grid: Crick
Photograph books of own life.
* Individual or class topic books.
* Unit A *Myself* topic books; Oxford Reading Trees. Pub: Oxford University Press.
See also other topic books in this series, e.g. *Houses and Homes*. Pub: Oxford University Press.

WORD LEVEL: HANDWRITING

W.L. YR: LO 12

To use a comfortable and efficient pencil grip.

See also: W.L. YR: LO 13, 14; S.L. YR: LO 3; T.L. YR: LO 11.4, 11.5; W.L. Yr 1 Term 1: LO 13, 14

Steps	Learning Objectives/Targets	Activities/Strategies	Assessment/IEP/Evaluation
P1–3	Experiences and responds to a range of different textures in multi-sensory environments.	In 1:1 in play situations to feel/handle/smell a range of different textures, e.g. pastas, jellies, clay, dough.	
P4	Shows interest in making marks in sand, on paper with paint, pens, pencils by holding implements with support.	Individually to mould, squeeze, cut, shape explore, draw and paint a range of different textures to develop tactile awareness.	
P5	Makes recognisable marks with pens, paints, etc. by holding tools independently, e.g. scribbles using a revolving movement, makes straight lines.	Individually use building simple constructions, colouring, sand, water play, switch control to develop dexterity and develop fine and gross motor skills.	
P6	Recognises that tools need to be handled in a certain way. Uses fine motor grip to pick up small items.	Individually use pincer grips, pegs, picking up beads, threading, using felt pens and large pencils to develop fine motor skills.	
P7	Begins to use an appropriate grip to hold large writing, colouring and painting implements.	Continued free-play and structured activities to encourage arm on table and efficient pencil grip.	
P8	Holds pencil accurately to write name or draw.	Daily practice in pencil activities.	

Suggested books, other resources
Range of 'textures', e.g. pastas, jellies, clay, dough.
Range and variety of tactile media for fine motor control.
Range of media for moulding and shaping, e.g. dough, clay.
Peg boards, building construction equipment, switches, light pens, large pencils/crayons, paints.

WORD LEVEL: HANDWRITING

W.L. YR: LO 13

To produce a controlled line which supports letter formation.

See also: W.L. YR: LO 12, 14; T.L YR: LO 11.3, 11.4; W.L. Yr 1 Term 1: LO 13, 14

Steps	Learning Objectives/Targets	Activities/Strategies	Assessment/IEP/Evaluation
P1–3	Encounters and experiences and responds to a range of activities to encourage eye movements L → R.	Multi-sensory activities in which pupils are encouraged to look and follow lights and objects L → R.	
P4	Experience a range of activities that encourage L → R hand movement.	Adult working in 1:1 or small group uses books, stories and IT packages to show L → R sequences.	
P5	Shows interest and joins in with activities to develop tracing along a line with support.	Individually, use of multi-sensory equipment, light pens, sand, plasticine, drawing with fingers, with large brushes and pens.	
P6	Begins to trace over adult marks along a line using large pens, pencils and brushes. Scribbles.	Individually tracing over writing using large writing tools.	
P7	Traces over adult model using an appropriate pencil grip using different sized tools. Draws pictures with some recognisable features. Draws circles and shapes.	As above using smaller tools and with more refined grip.	
P8	Using visual and tactile coordination draws lines left to right appropriately. Draws recognisable pictures.	Individually uses pens/pencils to draw lines left to write without support, trace over writing, copy writing, match shapes/letters/pictures.	

Suggested books, other resources
Range of tactile materials.
Range of media for moulding and shaping, e.g. dough, clay, plasticine, switches.
Light pens, large brushes, paints, large pencils/pens/crayons, letter shapes, letter cards.

WORD LEVEL: HANDWRITING

W.L. YR: LO 14

To write letters using the correct sequence of movements.

See also: W.L. YR: LO 12, 13; S.L. YR: LO 3; T.L. YR: LO 11.4, 11.5; W.L. Yr 1 Term 1: LO 14

Steps	Learning Objectives/Targets	Activities/Strategies	Assessment/IEP/Evaluation
P7	Following W.L. YR: LO 13, draws lines correctly left to right, draws circles to join up, and draws lines top to bottom on request.	Teacher models correct way to draw pupils' shadows. Practice drawing lines and circles in sand, paper, on computer.	
P8	Writes own name using correct sequence of movements. Practices correct movements for each letter of the alphabet.	Individual continual and regular practice of copy writing of individual letters on paper, in sand, with paint.	

Suggested books, other resources
Range of tactile media; sand, paper, large brushes, paints, large pencils/pens/crayons. Letter shapes, letter cards.

Strand ▋2▋ Sentence Level Work: Reception

Grammar and punctuation

GRAMMATICAL AWARENESS
Learning Objectives

SENTENCE LEVEL: GRAMMATICAL AWARENESS

S.L. YR: LO 1

To expect written text to make sense and check for sense if it does not.

See also: T.L. YR: LO 2

Steps	Learning Objectives/Targets	Activities/Strategies	Resources
P1	i) Encounters and experiences a range of stories, rhymes and poems. ii) Shows awareness of adult voice by focusing for short periods as stories take place.	In class, teacher reads range of age-appropriate stories, rhymes and poems using multi-sensory approaches as necessary.	
P2	i) Responds to a range of stories, rhymes and poems by body movement, or vocalisation. ii) Begins to recognise familiar events, characters, voices in familiar stories and rhymes.	While reading teacher gives time and encouragement to enable pupils to respond. Repetitive familiar stories with range of characters.	
P3	i) Begins to participate in familiar repetitive stories, smiling and showing enjoyment. ii) Anticipates aspects of the story such as repetitive words or phrases by body movement/vocalisation.	Use picture/story books to read simple stories using own words/symbols and use emphasis to promote anticipation.	
P4	Shows interest in the content of known story by listening, looking, pointing, vocalising on request.	Adult shares pictures of big book with pupils and talks about story.	
P5	Begins to answer simple questions about stories and rhymes.	To use questions relating to simple stories they know to elicit understanding, e.g. 'Where, how, what, why, where?'.	
P6	Recognises when parts of a familiar text are missing by laughing or vocalising.	Using wrongly sequenced story and pictures with clear beginning, middle, end. Pupils to re-sequence story, pictures correctly.	
P7	Recognises that the order of a simple text or rhyme has been changed.	As above with increasing number of stories and opportunities to re-work sequences.	
P8	Indicates what is wrong with a story when it does not make sense, and explains how to put it right.	Adult provides wide range of jumbled stories, or wrong endings to enable consolidation of understanding.	

Suggested books, other resources

Jack in the Box and *No Lunchbox* by Miriam Simon and Julie Park. Pub: GINN. ISBN 0 602 25947 9.

*Firefighters by Barrie Wade. Pub: Collins. ISBN 0-00-301228-X.

Own photograph books.

Own topic books.

Story and picture sequence cards.

SENTENCE LEVEL: GRAMMATICAL AWARENESS

S.L. YR: LO 2

To use awareness of the grammar of a sentence to predict words during shared reading and when re-reading familiar stories.

See also: S.L. YR: LO 1

Steps	Learning Objectives/Targets	Activities/Strategies	Resources
P1	i) Encounters and experiences a wide range of familiar stories and rhymes. ii) Shows awareness of adult voice as stories are read.	Use picture/story books to read simple stories using own words/symbols.	Big books.
P2	i) Responds to familiar rhymes and stories by body or eye movements. ii) Recognises some familiar characters and stories. Smiles in response to events in story.	Use questions relating to simple stories they know to elicit understanding, e.g. 'Where was Teddy?'.	
P3	i) Participates in shared story by seeking eye contact, vocalising at appropriate times and pointing to pictures or characters in familiar story. ii) Anticipates the next part of a familiar story, or a familiar rhyme and shows through body movement or vocalisation an awareness of content.	As above using picture and vocal clues to encourage anticipation.	
P4	Shows interest in stories and rhymes, and begins to find where things are in pictures.	Opportunities for pupils to find pictures that are 'in', 'on' or 'under' other objects in pictures and real life.	
P5	Begins to show understanding of actions in stories.	Teacher and pupils use actions to elicit understanding of present. Action books, e.g. 'things I can do'.	

Suggested books, other resources
How do we get there? by Maureen Rotfey. Pub: Macmillan. ISBN 0-333-59233-6.
* *In a dark dark wood*. Aidan Warton (ed.). Pub: Ginn. ISBN 0 602 22641-4.
See also: Other books, i.e. '*Start with Rhymes*' Series. Pub: Ginn.
Miniatures and objects. Personal activity photograph books. Action books of visits. Weekend news books. Preposition cards. Appropriate language programme
Word Level 1–3, e.g. Derbyshire Language Scheme.

SENTENCE LEVEL: GRAMMATICAL AWARENESS

S.L. YR: LO 2 *cont.*

To use awareness of the grammar of a sentence to predict words during shared reading and when re-reading familiar stories.

See also: S.L. YR: LO 1

Steps	Learning Objectives/Targets	Activities/Strategies	Resources
P6	Shows understanding of past and future tenses and begins to predict words appropriately.	Pupils make activity books of 'Things I did yesterday', 'Things I will do tomorrow'.	
P7	Joins in with predicting the next words in a simple sentence, e.g. Teddy was . . . Jumping.	Make own books. Re-tell stories orally in groups. Use small books to re-tell stories. Share news.	
P8	Predicts words in more complex sentences showing awareness of grammar, e.g. A big . . . was running . . . the stairs.	Whole group activities in which pupils take turns to complete and predict words in sentences.	

Suggested books, other resources

How do we get there? by Maureen Rotfey. Pub: Macmillan. ISBN 0-333-59233-6.
* *In a dark dark wood*, Aidan Warton (ed.). Pub: Ginn. ISBN 0 602 22641-4.
See also: Other books, i.e. *'Start with Rhymes'* Series. Pub: Ginn.
Miniatures and objects. Personal activity photograph books. Action books of visits. Weekend news books. Preposition cards. Appropriate language programme
Word Level 1–3, e.g. Derbyshire Language Scheme.

SENTENCE LEVEL: GRAMMATICAL AWARENESS

S.L. YR: LO 3

To know that words are ordered from left to right and need to be read that way to make sense.

See also: W.L. YR: LO 12, 13; T.L. YR: LO 1.4

Steps	Learning Objectives/Targets	Activities/Strategies	Resources
P1	i) Encounters and experiences range of activities to encourage L → R eye movements. May show reflex actions. ii) Shows awareness of activities in sensory rooms and environments by moving head, body, or vocalising.	In 1:1 or small group adult uses of a wide range of tactile and picture resources, including IT packages to guide pupil's hand/finger/eye sequencing.	
P2	i) Responds to activities by focusing consistently on moving objects. ii) Cooperates in sensory environments by waiting, looking, and communicating in some way.	Toy play activities with cars, etc., moving left to right.	
P3	i) Participates in activities in the sensory room and begins to follow with eyes. ii) Anticipates left to right movements by moving eyes in response to action or noise.	Using picture stories, adult guides pupil's hand/finger/eye, or makes noises for pupil to follow.	
P4	Shows interest in tracking toys, lights and pictures left to right. Copies others, listens and responds to instructions to 'follow'.	In small groups, pupils follow a picture/symbol story from left to right with finger/eye/IT.	
P5	Begins to look for pictures in a large text. Follows simple story as adult points to text and pictures left to right.	Look at books with adults and help with turning the pages. Make own picture books.	

Suggested books, other resources
The Toys Party by Roderick Hunt. Pub: Oxford Reading Tree. ISBN 0199 161 39 9.
See also: Other stories in Stage 2.
* *Today is Monday* by Eric Carte; Kaleidoscope Books. Pub: Puffin. ISBN 0-14-055310-X.
Sequenced sentences and pictures. Cars/lorries. Class photographs as story books.

SENTENCE LEVEL: GRAMMATICAL AWARENESS

S.L. YR: LO 3 *cont.*

To know that words are ordered from left to right and need to be read that way to make sense.

See also: W.L. YR: LO 12, 13; T.L. YR: LO 1.4

Steps	Learning Objectives/Targets	Activities/Strategies	Resources
P6	Recognises that the pictures on the left come before the pictures on the right.	Use of simple pictures in sequence of own life, e.g. dressing. Use of clearly sequenced picture books with adult pointing out sequence.	
P7	Joins in with sharing a simple story following words as adult points.	Simple texts as above.	
P8	Is aware that the print on the left page comes before print on the right.	Use of simple books and continual reminders and questions about left to right print.	

Suggested books, other resources
The Toys Party by Roderick Hunt. Pub: Oxford Reading Tree. ISBN 0199 161 39 9.
See also: Other stories in Stage 2.
* *Today is Monday* by Eric Carte; Kaleidoscope Books. Pub: Puffin. ISBN 0-14-055310-X.
Sequenced sentences and pictures. Cars/lorries. Class photographs as story books.

SENTENCE LEVEL: GRAMMATICAL AWARENESS

S.L. YR: LO 4

To use a capital letter for the start of own name.

See also: W.L. YR: LO 2.1, 3.1, 8, 12, 13, 14; T.L. YR: LO 12.2

Steps	Learning Objectives/Targets	Activities/Strategies	Resources
P1	i) Encounters and experiences a range of opportunities to hear own name such as registrations. ii) Shows awareness of hearing own name as part of a group.	In whole class discussion teacher calls names and waits for response. Reinforcement through daily routines such as registration, dinner register, group activities.	
P2	i) Responds to own name by body movement or eye movement. ii) Vocalises or shows recognition consistently when name is called. Shows pleasure.	Using the same activities as above teacher uses name card / symbol card first as reinforcement, then on its own.	
P3	i) Begins to communicate intentionally on hearing own name. Shows understanding of daily registration routine. ii) Anticipates hearing own name called in whole group situation. Shows anticipation by body / facial movements.	'Good morning' sessions with word cards / symbols and consistent order of calling names.	
P4	Shows interest in own name card and joins in with trying to find it. Begins to trace over large initial letter with finger, with adult support.	Tracing, over-writing activities using multi-sensory approaches.	
P5	Begins to recognise own name / symbol card and points to own initial letter. Traces over name card.	1:1 work to identify initial letter in different settings.	

Suggested books, other resources
Goldilocks. Pub: Ginn. ISBN 602 28055 9.
* *Zomo the Rabbit* by Gerald McDermott (ed.); Harcourt Brace. ISBN 0-15-201 011-4.
Letter Cluster Books.
Alphabet starter. Pub: Folens. Own name cards. Class words and class books.

SENTENCE LEVEL: GRAMMATICAL AWARENESS

S.L. YR: LO 4 *cont.*

To use a capital letter for the start of own name.

See also: W.L. YR: LO 2.1, 3.1, 8, 12, 13, 14; T.L. YR: LO 12.2

Steps	Learning Objectives/Targets	Activities/Strategies	Resources
P6	Recognises and begins to form own initial letter in a range of tactile ways.	Multi-sensory activities in whole class or 1:1.	
P7	Begins to find own initial letter of own name in a range of circumstances.	Using large pens and pencils for daily practise in recognising and writing own initial letter.	
P8	Uses correct initial letter for own name, orientating it accurately.	As above.	

Suggested books, other resources
Goldilocks. Pub: Ginn. ISBN 602 28055 9.
* *Zomo the Rabbit* by Gerald McDermott (ed.); Harcourt Brace. ISBN 0-15-201 011-4.
Letter Cluster Books.
Alphabet starter. Pub: Folens. Own name cards. Class words and class books.

Strand ⬛3 Text Level Work: Reception

Comprehension and composition

READING: UNDERSTANDING OF PRINT
Learning Objectives

READING: COMPREHENSION
Learning Objectives

WRITING: UNDERSTANDING OF PRINT
Learning Objectives

WRITING: COMPOSITION
Learning Objectives

TEXT LEVEL: READING: UNDERSTANDING OF PRINT

T.L. YR: LO 1.1

Through shared reading to recognise printed and handwritten words in a variety of settings.

See also: W.L. YR: LO 5, 6, 7, 8

Steps	Learning Objectives/Targets	Activities/Strategies	Resources
P1	i) Encounters and experiences a range of objects, both real and multi-sensory objects. ii) Shows awareness of everyday objects and begins to focus on some for short periods.	In whole class or group sessions such as speech/language sessions pupils handle a whole range of everyday objects. Also in multi-sensory environments.	
P2	i) Responds in some way to the above experiences, shows interest by exploring. ii) Cooperates with shared exploration of familiar objects, shows pleasure at particular ones.	Use a range of everyday objects/multi-sensory experiences linked to stories either in whole class, group or 1:1 to encourage looking and listening and elicit recognition.	
P3	i) Points to or eye points towards required toy or object, explores by feeling, turning, throwing, etc. ii) Anticipates getting hold of objects during whole class time, story time and shared text time, by looking or by body movement.	Encourage looking and listening by using a range of everyday objects linked to the story, in whole class, group or 1:1 to teach names and signs.	
P4	Shows interest in miniatures of everyday objects and transfer, that recognition to other examples of the same objects, e.g. a cup is always a cup.	Use miniature/model examples of the same objects, e.g. cups, chairs in doll's house, play areas of different sizes, shapes and colours.	
P5	Matching activities of pictures, photographs, miniatures and objects, name cards.	Shows understanding that the pictures and objects represent the same thing. Understands that own name card is different from others and begins to recognise own.	

Suggested books, other resources
Clicker with appropriate ready made or self made grid: Crick.
The Gingerbread Man by Brenda Parkes and Judith Smith. Pub: Rigby. ISBN 07312 10441.
* *Unit C Houses and Homes Topic Book.* Pub: Oxford Reading Tree. Also topic books in this series.
Collections of objects related to pictures and word cards/symbols to match objects, listening games, e.g. LDA tapes, sound lotto.
Language programme, e.g, Derbyshire Language Scheme.

TEXT LEVEL: READING: UNDERSTANDING OF PRINT

T.L. YR: LO 1.1 *cont.*

Through shared reading to recognise printed and handwritten words in a variety of settings.

See also: W.L. YR: LO 5, 6, 7, 8

Steps	Learning Objectives/Targets	Activities/Strategies	Resources
P6	Recognises photos or pictures of familiar objects and begins to name/sign them. Recognises own name.	Matching activities of photo/word or symbol to object. Own photo books, name cards.	
P7	Joins in with 'reading' simple photo books, class story books and class topic books. Joins in with reading daily 'news', shows understanding that the words mean something.	Matching activities of pupil's name to photograph, or simple words or symbols to names of objects round the classroom to other pupils, classroom furniture, labels, and simple topic books.	
P8	Reads simple text and 'news' in whole class times. Reads some labels and words independently and knows that they have meaning.	As above with extended opportunities to share text and written words, e.g. adult modelling writing on board.	

Suggested books, other resources
Clicker with appropriate ready made or self made grid: Crick.
The Gingerbread Man by Brenda Parkes and Judith Smith. Pub: Rigby. ISBN 07312 10441.
* *Unit C Houses and Homes Topic Book.* Pub: Oxford Reading Tree. Also topic books in this series.
Collections of objects related to pictures and word cards/symbols to match objects, listening games, e.g. LDA tapes, sound lotto.
Language programme, e.g. Derbyshire Language Scheme.

TEXT LEVEL: READING: UNDERSTANDING OF PRINT

T.L. YR: LO 1.2

Through shared reading to recognise that words can be written down to be read again for a wide range of purposes.

See also: T.L. YR: LO 11.1, 11.2

Steps	Learning Objectives/Targets	Activities/Strategies	Resources
P1	As LO 1.1. i) Encounters and experiences and enjoys a wide range of stories, poems and rhymes. ii) Shows awareness of adult reading different stories and rhymes.	Adult working individually in class or group indicates pictures or related 3D objects while reading range of stories, poems and rhymes.	
P2	i) Responds in some way to stories and objects, begins to explore as at 1.1. ii) Recognises familiar objects, and begins to recognise characters and familiar sayings in simple stories.	Adult uses picture or object stories, encouraging pupils to indicate choices for endings or things that might happen, e.g. 'Did the boy go to the beach?', while showing picture or show the picture of what happened.	
P3	i) Sustains interest in what happens next in stories, and in naming objects and characters. ii) Anticipates what might happen next during stories and class shared times.	In class and groups make collections of objects, including similar and different. 'What's this' and 'Where's Teddy' games.	
P4	Shows increasing interest in words and stories, and looks/feels for objects and sensory experiences.	Adult writes, and links simple words from story on flip chart and shows printed word/symbol, picture in book and other pictures/objects.	
P5	Begins to show understanding that a word or symbol relates to people or objects, e.g. name/symbol/photo cards.	Name cards. Make own simple books about collected objects using cut and stick exercises. Books to be shared with rest of class in plenary. Whole class shared news which adult writes on board.	

Suggested books, other resources
Clicker with appropriate ready made or self made grid: Crick.
The Duck in the Hat by Marvin Waddle; Pelican Big Book. Pub: Longman.
* *Not now Bernard* by David McKee; Pelican Big Book. Pub: Longman.
Collections of related objects, pictures, word cards/symbols. Own books.

TEXT LEVEL: READING: UNDERSTANDING OF PRINT

T.L. YR: LO 1.2 cont.

Through shared reading to recognise that words can be written down to be read again for a wide range of purposes.

See also: T.L. YR: LO 11.1, 11.2

Steps	Learning Objectives/Targets	Activities/Strategies	Resources
P6	Recognises some names and words on cards. Recognises own name when adult writes it on the board. Watches as adult writes a name and tries to guess as each letter is written.	In whole class times adults model writing by writing pupils' names as well as words linked to current story such as short extract such as 'Not now Bernard' (see below).	
P7	Joins in with reading words on the board as adult writes them. Suggests what some words are.	Increasing amount of adult modelling of words linked to stories and class activities, e.g. daily timetable.	
P8	Reads an increasing amount of words as adult writes them down and knows that they mean something.	As above, increasing and varying the content daily to provide for extension.	

Suggested books, other resources
Clicker with appropriate ready made or self made grid: Crick.
The Duck in the Hat by Marvin Waddle; Pelican Big Book. Pub: Longman.
* *Not now Bernard* by David McKee; Pelican Big Book. Pub: Longman.
Collections of related objects, pictures, word cards/symbols. Own books.

TEXT LEVEL: READING: UNDERSTANDING OF PRINT

T.L. YR: LO 1.3

Through shared reading to understand and use correctly terms about books and print.

See also: S.L. YR: LO 1

Steps	Learning Objectives/Targets	Activities/Strategies	Resources
P1	i) Encounters and experiences and enjoys a wide range of books and print. ii) Shows awareness of story time, and of when a story begins and ends.	Suitable texts in relation to age, multi-sensory activities, puppets, etc., to improve communication.	
P2	i) Responds to stories and rhymes in some way, may smile or focus on adult. ii) Recognises some familiar people and objects. Shows pleasure when a particular toy or object is shown which links to a story (object of reference).	Handling and looking at a range of books and objects with adults as part of shared whole class reading.	
P3	i) Points to familiar or favourite book or object to denote required story. ii) Anticipates the next part of a story or looks for objects out of sight.	Sequencing activities linked to whole class story. Daily time-table activities, e.g 'What comes next?'	
P4	Shows interest in books, and begins to handle them appropriately. Listens and responds to many stories.	Opportunities to handle books daily with individual time to share books with adults who talk about purpose of book as well as share stories.	
P5	Begins to turn pages on request. Points to pictures that interest them.	As above, with opportunities to learn specific names of parts of books, e.g. page, cover.	

Suggested books, other resources
Choice of Naughty Stories; Sherston.
The Three Little Pigs by Brenda Parkes and Judith Smith. Pub: Rigby. ISBN 07312 1043 3 (large) ISBN 07327 0539 8 (small).
* *Your amazing body* by Roderick Hunt. Pub: Oxford. ISBN 0-19-9166673-0.
See also Unit *A Myself*. Factfinders.
Own class and personal photograph books.
* Class and individual topic books.

TEXT LEVEL: READING: UNDERSTANDING OF PRINT

T.L. YR: LO 1.3 *cont.*

Through shared reading to understand and use correctly terms about books and print.

See also: S.L. YR: LO 1

Steps	Learning Objectives/Targets	Activities/Strategies	Resources
P6	Recognises and points to different types of information carrying tools, e.g. book, magazine, computer, newspaper. Names back, front, page, beginning, end.	Putting own books together in correct sequence.	
P7	Joins in with identifying particular aspects of books such as title, contents page, index.	As above, increasing questioning opportunities and exploration of different reading materials.	
P8	Indicates many aspects of books independently, knows about author, illustrator, where to begin, etc.	Opportunities to explain their knowledge and extend it by making their own books and including all aspects.	

Suggested books, other resources
Choice of Naughty Stories; Sherston.
The Three Little Pigs by Brenda Parkes and Judith Smith. Pub: Rigby. ISBN 07312 1043 3 (large) ISBN 07327 0539 8 (small).
* *Your amazing body* by Roderick Hunt. Pub: Oxford. ISBN 0-19-9166673-0.
See also Unit A *Myself.* Factfinders.
Own class and personal photograph books.
* Class and individual topic books.

TEXT LEVEL: READING: UNDERSTANDING OF PRINT

T.L. YR: LO 1.4

Through shared reading to track the text in the right order, page by page, left to right, top to bottom, while reading/telling a story and making one-to-one correspondences between written and spoken words.

See also: W.L. YR: LO 12, 13; S.L. YR: LO 3

Steps	Learning Objectives/Targets	Activities/Strategies	Resources
P1	i) Encounters and experiences a range of activities that encourage L → R eye movements and/or following L → R such as sensory room activities. ii) Shows awareness of different movements by focusing briefly as objects or lights are moved in front of pupil.	1:1 pupils use tracking activities, including IT packages, to consolidate L → R movements.	
P2	i) Responds in some way, with help, to activities to promote L → R eye and hand movements. ii) Recognises when an object is being moved and tries to follow.	In whole class or group pupils work with others to follow pictures, lights and moving toys, e.g. cars.	
P3	i) Sustains concentration for short periods as they participate in left to right activities. ii) Anticipates the next picture/object page by 'looking'.	Look at books with adults and help with turning the pages. Left to right orientation activities.	
P4	Shows interest in turning pages with adult, and looks for pictures as they do so. Knows when book is upside down.	Use of simple pictures in sequence of own life, e.g. dressing. Use of clearly sequenced picture books with adult pointing out sequence.	

Suggested books, other resources
Naughty stories. Oxford Reading Tree: Sherston.
Miss Mopples Washing Line by Anita Hewitt. ISBN 0-09-914411-5.
* *A day at our Dairy Farm* by Barbara Reeves. Pub: Modern Curriculum Press. ISBN 0-8136-1358-2.
Personal photograph books.
* Class or individual topic books.

TEXT LEVEL: READING: UNDERSTANDING OF PRINT

T.L. YR: LO 1.4 cont.

Through shared reading to track the text in the right order, page by page, left to right, top to bottom, while reading/telling a story and making one-to-one correspondences between written and spoken words.

See also: W.L. YR: LO 12, 13; S.L. YR: LO 3

Steps	Learning Objectives/Targets	Activities/Strategies	Resources
P5	Understands that pages are turned one at a time. Begins to do so carefully and independently. Follows simple stories as adult points. Turns pages to look at pictures.	Opportunities to turn the pages during story reading by adult. Find pictures within the story, searching a page at a time.	
P6	Follows a simple story with adults making a connection between spoken words. Recognises that pictures on the left come before pictures on the right.	In whole class, group or 1:1, pointing to words and pictures as story is read. Telling story in own words or symbols. Following while teacher tells story. Make own books with simple words/symbols.	
P7	Makes one-to-one correspondence with words on the page to those spoken by self and adult.	Adult and pupil point, using physical prompts to encourage 1:1 correspondence. Building up a story or sentence using single words.	
P8	Reads simple text and own books showing understanding of correct order. Shares more complex text with adult and knows that print is ordered left to right, and uses book appropriately to find words, pictures and simple information.	Wide range of opportunities to share different books.	

Suggested books, other resources
Naughty stories. Oxford Reading Tree: Sherston.
Miss Mopples Washing Line by Anita Hewitt. ISBN 0-09-914411-5.
* *A day at our Dairy Farm* by Barbara Reeves. Pub: Modern Curriculum Press. ISBN 0-8136-1358-2.
Personal photograph books.
* Class or individual topic books.

TEXT LEVEL. READING: COMPREHENSION

S.L. YR: LO 2

To use a variety of cues when reading; to show knowledge of the story and its context and awareness of how it should make sense grammatically.

See also: W.L. YR: LO 12, 13; S.L. YR: LO 3

Steps	Learning Objectives/Targets	Activities/Strategies	Resources
P1	i) Encounters and experiences a wide range of text, stories, rhymes as well as multi-sensory objects to help gain attention and eye contact. ii) Shows awareness of adult voice reading stories and focuses briefly on aspects.	Multi-sensory environments to promote attention. Wide range of stories, rhymes, puppets, etc.	
P2	i) Responds to stories, rhymes and objects by smiling or body movement. ii) Vocalises or gestures during stories, tries to communicate and respond to aspects of the story.	As above. Use question words, how, why, what, who, relating to simple stories they know to elicit understanding, e.g. 'Where was Teddy?'.	
P3	i) Sustains concentration as stories become familiar, smiles and watches as adult reads. ii) Anticipates what might come next in a rhyme or story, and 'looks for' missing objects that are hidden.	Practical activities with pupils encouraged to 'look' for objects, 'look at' pictures, touch puppets and respond to them.	
P4	Shows interest in short stories and anticipates or 'looks for' the next part of the story or rhyme. To show understanding of the grammatical content in relation to verbs.	Practical activities related to sharing stories and rhymes and talking about what happens. Personal sequential photograph books of pupils, e.g. putting coat on, riding my bike, taking coat off.	
P5	Begins to order activities both in everyday context and within simple text.	Daily timetable activities. Making activity/action books of visits, weekend news books in the past.	

Suggested books, other resources
Clicker with appropriate ready made or self made grid: Crick.
Bear Facts Music and lyrics by Norman L. Gentner (ed.); Wright Group. (Contains tapes to aid rhyming.) ISBN 0-7802-1264-9.
* *Superkids* by Brian and Jillian Curving. Sunshine Books: Heinemann.
See also: other books in Sunshine series: Heinemann.

TEXT LEVEL: READING: COMPREHENSION

S.L. YR: LO 2 *cont.*

To use a variety of cues when reading: to show knowledge of the story and its context and awareness of how it should make sense grammatically.

See also: W.L. YR: LO 12, 13; S.L. YR: LO 3

Steps	Learning Objectives/Targets	Activities/Strategies	Resources
P6	Recognises the correct sequence of timetable. Recognises the beginning, middle and end of a familiar story. Uses pictures to help understand stories.	As above. Make own books. Re-tell stories orally in groups. Use small books to re-tell stories. Share news. Build stories together.	
P7	Joins in with looking for clues in pictures to help with understanding the context. Finds names within simple text.	Reading own and others' photo books. Sharing topic books and simple text with adults and finding clues to help understanding.	
P8	Uses pictures, initial sounds, names to help understand the story.	Opportunities to share stories so that they can use their skills to look for clues and identify context of story.	

Suggested books, other resources
Clicker with appropriate ready made or self made grid: Crick.
Bear Facts Music and lyrics by Norman L. Gentner (ed.). Wright Group. (Contains tapes to aid rhymings.) ISBN 0-7802-1264-9.
* *Superkids* by Brian and Jillian Curving. Sunshine Books: Heinemann.
See also: other books in Sunshine series: Heinemann.

TEXT LEVEL: READING: COMPREHENSION

T.L. YR: LO 3

To re-read a text to provide context cues to help read unfamiliar words.

See also: W.L. YR: LO 12, 13; S.L. YR: LO 3

Steps	Learning Objectives/Targets	Activities/Strategies	Resources
P1	As LO 2. i) Encounters and experiences a range of simple stories as part of whole class shared text. ii) Shows awareness of adult and focuses for short periods during shared text time.	In whole class and group adult reads a wide range of stories and uses questioning, picture and symbol cues to consolidate understanding and encourage discussion.	
P2	i) Responds in some way to simple stories and shows interest in some parts, and in adult voice. ii) Shows pleasure in familiar stories. Tries to communicate responses to the adult and to the story.	Adults encourage listening by reading simple familiar stories.	
P3	i) Uses gestures, vocalisations or eye contact to try to participate in the story and questions. ii) Anticipates familiar parts of story or rhyme as adult reads.	Use familiar pictures and texts to enable pupils to know when a part is missed out, or to indicate what comes next.	
P4	Shows interest in pictures as adult reads simple stories. Finds familiar picture on request.	In whole class, group, 1:1, pupils follow a story and look at pictures, or feel tactile pictures.	
P5	Begins to develop skills in using pictures to understand context of story. Follows story well.	Use of a range of known and unknown stories to match pictures to context.	

Suggested books, other resources
Naughty Stories. Oxford Reading Tree: Sherston.
The Lion and the Mouse re-told by Diana Bentley. Pub: Heinemann. ISBN 0435 090 304.
See also: Other books in 'Once upon a time' world series. Pub: Heinemann.
* *Red Bird* by David Orme. Pub: Collins. ISBN 0-00-301 230-1. Own stories with simple text.

TEXT LEVEL: READING: COMPREHENSION

T.L. YR: LO 3 *cont.*

To re-read a text to provide context cues to help read unfamiliar words.

See also: W.L. YR: LO 12, 13; S.L. YR: LO 3

Steps	Learning Objectives/Targets	Activities/Strategies	Resources
P6	Recognises how pictures illustrate and help to explain the story. Begins to use own reading skills to identify names of characters.	Word matching games of characters from stories. Sequential games using pictures from story to be read.	
P7	Joins in with finding clues to help understading during shared text time. Begins to look further on and back at pictures and words.	Adult focuses questions relating to context, e.g. questions and revisiting.	
P8	Uses text in simple stories to help understanding by looking for words further on, or back in the text and by using picture and content as clues.	Increasing opportunities to talk with others and adults about the context of print, 'who, where, how do you know, what', etc.	

Suggested books, other resources
Naughty Stories. Oxford Reading Tree: Sherston.
The Lion and the Mouse re-told by Diana Bentley. Pub: Heinemann. ISBN 0435 090 304.
See also: Other books in 'Once upon a time' world series. Pub: Heinemann.
* *Red Bird* by David Orme. Pub: Collins. ISBN 0-00-301 230-1. Own stories with simple text.

TEXT LEVEL: READING: COMPREHENSION

T.L. YR: LO 4

To notice the difference between spoken and written forms through re-telling known stories: to compose 'told' versions with what the book 'says'.

See also: T.L. YR: 1.2, 1.3, 3

Steps	Learning Objectives/Targets	Activities/Strategies	Resources
P1	As LO 2 and 3. i) Encounters and experiences listening to a wide range of 'told' stories and rhymes, as well as stories and rhymes that are read. ii) Shows awareness of story time and of adult.	In whole class teacher tells and reads a range of familiar stories.	
P2	i) Responds in some way to 'told' and 'read' stories through eye contact or body language. ii) Tries to communicate a response or answer to adult during story time.	Adult tells story without text/pictures, and also reads same printed stories.	
P3	i) Participates actively in told and read stories by gesturing or vocalising. Remembers some aspects of the story, particularly familiar repetitive parts. ii) Anticipates what comes next in told and read stories.	Opportunities created to enable pupils to anticipate content, e.g. pausing, questioning. Uses printed text of same story (above), reading word for word. Pupils join in.	
P4	Shows interest in both told and read stories by looking at pictures, anticipating and joining in with aspects of the stories.	Teacher uses a range of spoken/written stories (as above) to consolidate understanding, and uses questioning and discussion emphasising differences.	
P5	Begins to choose between told and read stories when asked to make a choice.	Opportunities for pupils to make choices of familiar told or read stories.	
P6	Recognises the difference between told and read versions of same story.	Pupils given opportunity to make valid choices, e.g. told and read versions of stories such as 'Three pigs', 'Three bears'.	
P7	Joins in with making suggestions about how to compose their own versions of familiar told story.	Whole class composing of told stories following familiar read story. Whole class book of own ideas for own version.	
P8	Re-tells stories they have read in own words.	Opportunities for re-telling individually.	

Suggested books, other resources
Naughty Stories. Oxford Reading Tree: Sherston.
Little Red Hen re-told by Brenda Parkes and Judith Smith. Pub: Kingscourt.

TEXT LEVEL: READING: COMPREHENSION

T.L. YR: LO 5

To understand how story book language works and to use some of the formal elements when re-telling stories.

See also: T.L. YR: LO 4

Steps	Learning Objectives/Targets	Activities/Strategies	Resources
P1	From LO 2, 3 and 4. i) Encounters and experiences range of stories containing formal elements. ii) Focuses attention on adult and appears ready to contribute during shared text time.	In whole class, adult reads/tells a range of familiar stories emphasising the formal elements, e.g. 'Once upon a time', 'happily ever after'.	
P2	i) Responds in some way to range of familiar stories containing formal elements. ii) Tries to communicate in some way as familiar stories are told.	Adult reads a simple story/stories of only three elements, a clear beginning, middle and end.	
P3	i) Requests favourite stories by pointing or gesturing in some way. Smiles as formal 'beginings' occur. ii) Anticipates and shows understanding of simple story using three formal elements.	Adult creates opportunities for anticipation by pausing, questioning and using real resources. Repetition of familiar story with emphasis on beginning and end.	
P4	Shows interest in all aspects of the story, and recognises 'beginning' and 'end'.	Emphasis on formal language at beginning and end of story.	
P5	Begins to indicate what happens at the beginning of a familiar story and what happens at the end.	Teacher uses the same activities as above emphasising beginning and end.	
P6	Recognises that a story has several parts. Joins in with 'Once upon a time' and 'happily ever after'.	Opportunities to indicate some phrases within stories, particularly familiar phrases.	
P7	Begins familiar story in own words, and tells other main aspects with beginning, middle and end.	Continual re-telling gradually building confidence in identifying aspects of stories as they become familiar.	
P8	Identifies beginning, middle and end of known stories, and begins to use appropriate formal elements when telling or re-telling stories, identifying them in less familiar situations.	Opportunities for pupils to use formal elements in their story telling.	

Suggested books, other resources
Naughty Stories. Oxford Reading Tree: Sherston.
Cinderella by Laszio Gal. Pub: Ginn. ISBN 0602 280 567 (large), ISBN 0602 280 532 (small).

TEXT LEVEL. READING: COMPREHENSION

T.L. YR: LO 6

To re-read frequently a variety of familiar texts.

See also: T.L. YR: LO 1.2, 1.3, 3, 4, 5

Steps	Learning Objectives/Targets	Activities/Strategies	Resources
P1	i) Encounters and experiences a wide range of familiar texts. ii) Shows some awareness of favourite repetitive and familiar stories.	In whole class adult reads and re-reads a wide range of familiar texts, using different formats.	
P2	i) Responds positively to a story by smiling, eye contact or a stillness, a recognition that something is happening. ii) Tries to interact with aspects of familiar stories.	Teacher reads and re-reads a variety of familiar texts, e.g. Big books, story books, taped stories with texts, poems, wall stories.	
P3	i) Sustains concentration particularly when familiar stories have a repetitive phrase, e.g. traditional tales. ii) Anticipates what comes next in a story that is familiar and responds accordingly.	Teacher reads a familiar story and prompts with question or pauses with gesture to elicit response or anticipation.	
P4	Begins to show interest and join in with sounds, words or gestures.	Teacher reads a familiar story and encourages pupils to join in at appropriate time.	
P5	Listens well. Begins to show that they are aware when a story is changed, when something is missing or content different. Recognises pictures.	Adult and pupil share story together and pupil indicates changes, pictures characters through words, symbols and gestures, pointing.	
P6	Recognises that the story is always the same if read from the same book. Identifies familiar names or letters.	Adult and pupil turn pages together. Adult encourages vocalisation and re-telling.	
P7	Joins in with reading in own words, reading written text where possible.	Individually or in small group adult encourages pupils to identify and read familiar words.	
P8	Re-reads simple text.	In small groups pupils share texts that are familiar and re-read.	

Suggested books, other resources
What can you see? by Wendy Body. Pelican Big Books. Pub: Longman.
* *Dragon's Song* by Jan Mike. Pub: Modern Curriculum Press. ISBN 0-8136-1181-4.

TEXT LEVEL: READING: COMPREHENSION

T.L. YR: LO 7

To use knowledge of familiar texts to re-enact or re-tell to others, recounting the main points in the correct sequence.

See also: T.L. YR: LO 10, 14

Steps	Learning Objectives/Targets	Activities/Strategies	Resources
P1	i) Encounters and experiences a range of stories and rhymes with adult using puppets or characters to tell the story. ii) Shows awareness of stories, focusing on objects, puppets, etc.	In whole class or groups adult uses puppets, dolls or toys to represent at least part of a story.	
P2	i) Responds in some way to a story/several stories with dramatic input. ii) Tries to interact with puppets and parts of the story by vocalising, gesturing, becoming excited.	Adult dramatises story/stories with a clear beginning, middle and end.	
P3	i) Gestures and gains eye contact as they try to interact with the story. ii) Anticipates things that might happen in the story as puppets enact while adult reads or tells.	Pupils enabled to enjoy and watch puppets enacting stories in many situations.	
P4	Shows interest in re-enactment by trying to hold puppets or laughing/touching as story takes place.	In small groups, pupils work together/watch adults to re-create parts of stories using a range of artefacts/objects/resources/puppets.	
P5	Begins to use puppets themselves, vocalising for them.	Many opportunities to use puppets to show others what they can do/tell about their day.	
P6	Recognises that puppets can tell a story, tries to do this in own way.	Group work with adult to organise a puppet show about stories they have heard.	
P7	Joins in with others to create a puppet display, or dramatic representation of a familiar story.	As above, also using drama.	
P8	Is able to re-enact familiar stories with beginning, middle and end.	Work in groups to practise and improve performances of stories they have heard. Perform for others.	

Suggested books, other resources
Naughty Stories. Oxford Reading Tree: Sherston.
The Enormous Watermelon by Brenda Parkes and Judith Smith. Pub: Kingscourt.
* *The Three Billy Goats Gruff* re-told by Judith Smith and Brenda Parkes. Pub: Kingscourt.
Range of puppets, toys to represent own class story or familiar story.

TEXT LEVEL: READING: COMPREHENSION

T.L. YR: LO 8

To locate and read significant parts of the text, names of key characters, rhymes and chants, speech bubbles, italicised, enlarged words.

See also: T.L. YR: LO 1.2, 1.3, 3, 4, 5, 6

Steps	Learning Objectives/Targets	Activities/Strategies	Resources
P1–3	As LO 2–7. Encounters and experiences a range of stories which contain rhymes/chants in which key characters are easily anticipated and identified. Awareness and responses elicited through adult interaction and use of puppets, objects of reference, key characters.	In class group teacher reads familiar texts, emphasising rhymes, chants and when key characters are mentioned.	
P4	Listens and responds to many different stories with range of characters. Locates the same character on different pages.	Teacher reads Big book stories until pupils become very familiar with them, encouraging them to look at pictures and comment.	
P5	Begins to find key pictures in books and identify features within the pictures . Joins in at appropriate time with significant parts of a text, verbally, by vocalisation or gesture.	Range of adult/pupil interactions relating to stories with strong or interesting characters.	
P6	Recognises familiar parts of stories and points to familiar words/names in text. Joins in with story by reading words or names. Knows where speech bubbles are. Recognises different print types with emphasis.	Teacher reads familiar Big book, indicates word or phrase and waits for pupils to join in with words, signs or sounds.	
P7	Reads names, phrases consistently in simple text. Recognises initial letter/sound or whole word. Reads speech bubbles.	Teacher focuses pupils on planned character name or initial letter/sound, word.	
P8	Reads simple stories including names, speech bubbles and emphasising where appropriate.	Opportunities to read and re-read familiar texts with character names, speech bubbles, chants, etc.	

Suggested books, other resources
Grandma and Me: REM.
See also: *Living books series.*
Little Miss Muffet. Pub: Ginn. ISBN 602 28040 0
Own photograph/picture stories.
* *Don't forget the Bacon* by Pat Hutchins. Pub: Mulberry Big Books. ISB 0-688-13102-6.

TEXT LEVEL: READING: COMPREHENSION

T.L. YR: LO 9

To be aware of story structures and the ways that stories are built up and concluded.

See also: T.L. YR: LO 1.2, 1.3, 3, 4, 5, 6, 8

Steps	Learning Objectives/Targets	Activities/Strategies	Resources
P1–3	From LO 2–8. Encounters and experiences a wide range of stories with clear beginning, middle and end and has opportunities to respond through body movement or eye pointing, anticipating aspects of story.	In whole class, adult uses multi-sensory approaches and a wide range of stories with clear, sound, structure and uses discussion, picture stories to emphasise structure, encourage responses and anticipation.	
P4	Shows interest in simple structure of stories, e.g. actions, reactions, consequences.	In whole class, group or individually. Use of simple stories with clear beginning, middle and end. Sequencing activities with pictures or words to reflect action, reaction and consequence, e.g. 'I fell over', 'I hurt my knee', 'I cried'.	
P5	Shows understanding of the need for a beginning and an end, and joins in with suggestions.	Work in small groups or individually to tell own news, make own books, use sequencing activities with pictures or words.	
P6	Recognises the shape of stories and talks about the different elements.	Make up a group story, taking turns showing what happened first, the reaction and the consequences.	
P7	Able to sequence picture stories and pictures with simple text.	Sequences of picture and text stories for pupils to order and talk about.	
P8	Identifies how a story is built up. Sequences own stories.	More complex sequencing activities.	

Suggested books, other resources
Arthur's birthday: REM.
See also: *Living book series*.
Mr Grumpy's Outing by John Burmingham. Pub: Henry Holt. ISBN 0-8050-3854-X.
* *Be Quiet* by Dina Anastasio. Pub: Modern Curriculum Press. ISBN 0-8130-1338-8.
Picture stories, action/reaction/consequence cards.

TEXT LEVEL: READING: COMPREHENSION

T.L. YR: LO 10

To re-read and recite stories and rhymes with predictable and repeated patterns and experiment with similar rhyming patterns.

See also: T.L. YR: LO 1.1, 1.2

Steps	Learning Objectives/Targets	Activities/Strategies	Resources
P1–2	From LO 2–9. Encounters and experiences and responds to stories and rhymes with predictable and repeated patterns within whole class and individual sessions.	Adult reads and re-reads a range of age appropriate stories with predictable patterns, e.g. Three pigs, Three bears. Responses and interactions encouraged and fostered.	
P3	i) Tries to communicate and participate in particular repetitive phrases. ii) Anticipates familiar parts of rhymes and stories, verbally, by vocalisation or gesture.	Adult reads familiar rhymes and stories, ensuring opportunities for response.	
P4	Shows interest in familiar rhymes and stories verbally, by vocalisation or gesture. Turns pages and looks for what comes next.	Adult reads/tells familiar rhymes and stories and encourages pupils to join where appropriate.	
P5	Begins to predict/state what comes next in familiar rhymes/stories and rhymes. Claps to rhythm and rhyme in story.	In whole class, small group or individually use re-telling, actions, pictures or words/symbols to re-tell whole story.	
P6	Re-tells part of rhyme/story in correct sequence. Identifies names of characters, and some letter sounds, and says words that rhyme.	In small groups sequence part of story using actions, pictures or words/symbols. Small group sequences put together to make whole story and identify rhymimg words.	
P7	Joins in with re-telling parts of story or rhyme, particularly the important features, including chants. Begins to read familiar names, chants and jingles. Identifies rhyming words that sound the same as those in the story.	In whole class, small groups or individually use re-telling actions, pictures or words/symbols to re-tell whole story and recognise and find rhyming words.	
P8	Reads simple rhyme or story and makes lists of words that rhyme, changing some words in the story to see what happens.	In whole class or individually teacher points to individual words/phrases as pupil reads, identifies rhymes and writes them down.	

Suggested books, other resources
Rhyme and analogy activity. Softman: Sherston.
One Two Three Four by Claude Belanger. Pub: Kingscourt.
* *What do you see* by Judy Naylor. Pub: Modern Curriculum Press. ISBN 0-8136-1076-1 (large) ISBN 0-8136-1080-X (small).

97

TEXT LEVEL: WRITING: UNDERSTANDING OF PRINT

T.L. YR: LO 11.1

Through shared writing to understand that writing can be used for a range of purposes.

See also: T.L. YR: LO 1.1, 1.2

Steps	Learning Objectives/Targets	Activities/Strategies	Resources
P1–3	Encounters and experiences a range of activities in which they observe adults writing for a purpose. Has opportunities to respond to a wide range of tactile activities to develop use of hands.	Shared writing experiences as adult writes on board. Multi-sensory activities including sensory room, switches to achieve cause/effect. In class a range of exploration activities with pasta, jelly, dough, water and sand to promote tactile responses and enjoyment.	
P4	Knows that their action on something causes a response. Uses hands to make marks on paper with paint, etc. Observes as adult writes captions to pictures.	Cause/effect toys. Adult models writing for different purposes, e.g. daily timetables, jobs, captions.	
P5	Shows understanding that writing or symbols can be used to describe something, e.g. name cards, names on own pictures, timetables. Scribbles news.	Matching activities or pupil's name to photograph, or simple words or symbols to names of objects round the classroom. Attempts own writing. Range of scribble/drawing/painting.	
P6	Recognises that words or symbols can be used to carry a message and needs to be written down. Helps to add to shared writing by offering comments.	Taking messages around the school, and taking notes and diaries home. Adult reading what parents have written so that pupils can see the writing.	
P7	Begins to make marks on paper that are recognisable to tell news, write name, take a message. Understands that what the adult writes on the board means something.	Matching symbols to word of everyday activities/objects, e.g. Timetable, home-school books/classroom tasks/messages. Writes news and name.	
P8	Knows that writing is used for different purposes such as timetables, jobs, lists, naming.	Involvement in whole class times when writing is used to describe events, activities, objects, people.	

Suggested books, other resources
Talking Write Away: Black Cat.
Dear Daddy by Philippe Dupasquier. Pelican Big Book. Pub: Longman. ISBN 0582 333504 (large) ISBN 0582 339461 (small).
* *When the circus comes to town* by Brenda Parkes. Pub: Kingscourt.
Objects and name cards. Photographs and name cards. Communication boards. Symbols/word cards for everyday objects. Pen-friends.

TEXT LEVEL: WRITING: UNDERSTANDING OF PRINT

T.L. YR: LO 11.2

Through shared writing to understand that writing remains constant.

See also: T.L. YR: LO 1.2, 1.3, 3, 4, 5, 6, 8

Steps	Learning Objectives/Targets	Activities/Strategies	Resources
P1–3	Encounters and experiences many activities linked to stories, rhymes and objects. Experiences multi-sensory activities to promote constancy of objects. Develops responses and anticipation of own objects.	Pupil is shown, touches, chooses, own objects in daily activities. Exploration of constancy of objects, e.g. hide and seek games, 'where is the . . .'.	
P4	Shows interest as adult writes names and captions during shared writing time.	Regular modelling by adult of writing pupils' names and names of objects that are familiar. Use of words/symbols for miniatures, models, collections of the same objects to reinforce concept of constancy.	
P5	Shows understanding that words or symbols identify people and objects.	Class 'hello' games. Word and symbol matching with classroom objects.	
P6	Recognises that own name begins with a certain letter and always does. Recognises that other people's names are different.	Continuous observation of modelling in shared writing times of names of pupils and objects.	
P7	Chooses initials for pupils and objects as adult writes. Understands that they never change.	As above, increasing the opportunities to see writing related to people and objects.	
P8	Understands that the written word for people and objects does not change.	Increased opportunities to observe shared writing.	

Suggested books, other resources
Clicker with appropriate ready made or self made grid: Crick.
Pupil name/symbol cards. Word/symbol of constant classroom items. Miniatures with word/symbols. Collection of same objects, e.g. Teddies.

TEXT LEVEL: WRITING: UNDERSTANDING OF PRINT

T.L. YR: LO 11.3

Through shared writing to distinguish between writing and drawing in books and in own work.

See also: T.L. YR: LO 1.2, 1.3, 3, 4, 5, 6, 8

Steps	Learning Objectives/Targets	Activities/Strategies	Resources
P1–3	Encounters and experiences many pre-writing activities and shared stories from previous LO's and has opportunities to respond to shared writing and drawing activities in which adults model, or they themselves explore, investigate and find.	In whole class sessions teacher uses white board or flip chart to write/draw with pupils, talking about purposes. Multi-sensory activities such as feeling or searching in pasta, jelly, sand, water to develop understanding of objects and develop hand control.	
P4	Shows awareness of pictures/drawings/writing/symbols by looking, vocalising, touching.	In whole class or small group sessions, pupils share with adult a range of books and talk about the 'purpose' of writing/drawing.	
P5	Recognises that pictures/photos and symbols show what things are like, i.e. the same.	Make whole class book in which pupils draw and teacher writes the caption. Use of whole class discussion to point out the meaning of both.	
P6	Recognises that pictures can be used to represent objects.	To develop individual news picture books in which adult writes captions. Discussion about differences between pictures and words.	
P7	Joins in with choosing pictures/photos to match a word on the board.	Whole class shared time in which pupils have photos or pictures to choose from as adult writes.	
P8	Recognises that pictures are different from words and that both show or tell what things are like.	Whole class and individual drawings and news times.	

Suggested books, other resources
Talking Write Away: Black Cat.
Whole class books. News pictures. Letter/Word cards.

TEXT LEVEL: WRITING: UNDERSTANDING OF PRINT

T.L. YR: LO 11.4

To understand how writing is formed directionally, a word at a time.

See also: W.L. YR: LO 8, 12, 13, 14; S.L. YR: LO 3

Steps	Learning Objectives/Targets	Activities/Strategies	Resources
P1–3	As LO 11.1, 11.2, 11.3. Encounters and experiences and has opportunities to respond to a wide range of tactile media to encourage hand movements.	In 1:1 use a range of media, multi-sensory activities, massages, tactile objects, switches to promote tactile awareness and anticipation of temperature and texture.	
P4	Shows interest in adult writing in shared times, and in exploration of tactile media. Hand painting.	In small groups arrange tactile experiences as well as observation of adult models	
P5	Makes marks on paper with large pens, brushes and tries to copy adult models.	In 1:1, adult makes marks on paper, pupil copies marks. Adult make marks in sand/on paper. Pupil traces over marks.	
P6	Recognises own initial letter and tries to trace over it. Uses finger to trace over name and begins to write it.	Frequent over-writing activities with initial starting point identified.	
P7	Writes initial letter of name accurately. Copies own name and other words correctly.	Daily practice in copying own name with initial starting point identified.	
P8	Writes own name correctly and begins to form other words directionally correct into simple sentences.	Practice in guided writing activities. Opportunities to copy good models regularly.	

Suggested books, other resources
Range of tactile media, e.g. dough, clay, jelly, pasta. Large pens/pencils/crayons/brushes/paints. Name cards. Initial letter cards. Word lists. Sand tray, light pen.

TEXT LEVEL: WRITING: UNDERSTANDING OF PRINT

T.L. YR: LO 11.5

Through shared writing to understand how letters are formed and used to spell words.

See also: W.L. YR: LO 8, 12, 13, 14; S.L. YR: LO 3; T.L. YR LO 11.4

Steps	Learning Objectives/Targets	Activities/Strategies	Resources
P1–3	As LO 11.1, 11.2, 11.3, 11.4. Encounters and experiences and has opportunities to respond to a range of sensory activities to promote tactile awareness.	Wide range of multi-sensory activities, including independent free play with sand, dough, paint, with support to make marks.	
P4	Shows interest in observing adult modelling of writing in shared times. Uses tactile media to mould and shape materials. Uses tools to make marks with paint.	On an individual basis pupils encouraged to take part in continued range of observation/drawing/writing/painting activities.	
P5	Makes marks and tries to copy adult models. Writes own letter shapes in the air and copies sound.	Use a range of equipment, e.g. multi-sensory, sand, light pencils, plasticine to form letters/practise direction while saying sound.	
P6	Copies adult model of own name correctly. Traces and attempts to write independently, making initial letter accurately while saying sound.	With adult help identify words beginning with own letter and make them in the air, on paper, in sand, etc., focusing on sound and direction.	
P7	Finds other words beginning with own letter sound. Attempts to say the word by using initial sound. Writes initial sound and attempts others. Uses simple word and phonic cards to identify sounds and build words.	In 1:1, say sound of own letter while reading words beginning with it. Writes words beginning with own letter sound.	
P8	Writes an increasing number of words that are phonetically correct. Uses simple word books to identify letter sounds. Uses adult models to help correct orientation. Begins to write news and stories that are phonetically accurate.	In 1:1 or in small group, identify initial letter sounds and use them in writing words, e.g. ball, bat, bee.	

Suggested books, other resources

Range and sensory and tactile resources to encourage exploration and fine motor control, e.g. sand, light, pens, plasticine. Name/word cards. Letter cards. Pictures, captions. Tracing and over-writing activities. Using whole class/group session, teacher writes while pupils watch, ensuring correct direction and formation of letters. Group sessions in building words together, i.e. word cards, pictures, captions. During whole class sessions use pictures to support writing of simple words.

TEXT LEVEL. WRITING: COMPOSITION

T.L. YR: LO 11.6

Through shared writing to apply knowledge of letter/sound correspondences in helping the teacher to scribe, and re-reading what the class has written.

See also: W.L. YR: LO 8, 12, 13, 14; S.L. YR: LO 3; T.L. YR: LO 11.4 refer to LO 12.4

Steps	Learning Objectives/Targets	Activities/Strategies	Resources
P1	i) Encounters and experiences many different sounds in a range of ways, particularly own name sound. ii) Shows awareness of sounds and of own name.	Adult uses range of sound games and activities to ensure pupils develop awareness of different noises.	
P2	i) Responds to sounds by body movement or vocalising. Tries to communicate as a response to different sounds and own name. ii) Makes a consistent response and begins to show preferences.	In whole class session, pupils and adults share sounds and noises and comment, encouraging a response.	
P3	i) Sustains interest and concentration when listening to story tapes, music tapes, or stories and rhymes. ii) Anticipates a sound in a game or on a tape. Looks towards dinner trolley/piano, etc. Smiles when name is called.	As above, encouraging pupils to anticipate by repeating the activity or by pausing/waiting, etc.	
P4	Knows own name and shows interest in initial letter sound. Tries to say name and sound.	Use flip chart to write story or news with pupils helping to make own initial sounds and correct mistakes.	
P5	Begins to recognise own initial letter when written down. Says the sound as adult writes. Begins to find it in other words.	As above, with opportunities to identify sounds/letters connected with own names, using blends as appropriate.	
P6	Attempts to say the initial sound of several familiar words as adult scribes.	Whole class shared writing times when pupils can take turns to identify letters and sounds.	
P7	Joins in with saying final sounds to simple CVC words as adult scribes. Joins in with reading simple CVC words that the class has written.	As above, with adult emphasising initial and final sounds.	
P8	Spells simple words accurately as adult writes. Uses knowledge of sound/letter correspondence to build unknown words. Reads back simple text.	Increased opportunities for shared writing and reading back.	

Suggested books, other resources
Talking Write Away: Black Cat. Single and blend letter cards, e.g. LDA. Sound games, e.g. sound lotto. Daily news in groups. Teacher scribes.

TEXT LEVEL: WRITING: COMPOSITION

T.L. YR: LO 12.1

Through guided and independent writing to experiment with writing in a variety of play, exploratory and role-play situations.

Steps	Learning Objectives/Targets	Activities/Strategies	Resources
P1–3	As previous T.L. LO's. Encounters and experiences and has opportunities to respond to tactile materials to develop hand movements as earlier writing objectives.	Independent use of range of media to explore, search for objects, develop hand control and make marks.	
P4	Makes marks with simple tools as previously. Has experience of different kinds of writing in whole class shared times.	In whole class sessions, teacher indicates how writing helps us to understand or tell others about ourselves.	
P5	Begins to use a variety of play situations to extend writing skills, e.g. play house, post office, painting, colouring.	To use a range of equipment to deveop skills as role play with adult support.	
P6	Recognises writing around the classroom and in the community, e.g. menus, letters and news.	Play activities in classroom to encourage writing for fun, e.g. pen-friends. Visits to community.	
P7	Joins in with a wide range of writing activities such as sending messages, writing lists, menus.	Daily practice in writing for different purposes.	
P8	Writes regularly for a purpose in different role-play situations.	Setting up different areas and computer to promote writing for different reasons.	

Suggested books, other resources
Range of media to encourage writing or making marks on paper in play situations. Opportunities to play in home corner, etc., with range of media, puppets, etc. See also 7 YR 1.
First Workshop Database: Black Cat.
Little Meanie's Lunch — a play by Joy Cowley. Pub: Shortlands. ISBN 0-7901-1326-0.
See also 'Ready Set Go' books. Pub: Shortlands.
Puppets, toys, objects in play corner.
Letter/word/name cards.
Large pens/pencils/crayons/brushes.
Sand, light pen.

TEXT LEVEL: WRITING: COMPOSITION

T.L. YR: LO 12.2

Through guided and independent writing to write their own names.

See also: Section 1.5; 2.4 Refer to Section 1, no 5; Section 2, no 4

Steps	Learning Objectives/Targets	Activities/Strategies	Resources
P1	i) Encounters and experiences a range of multi-sensory activities in which pupils can move their hands/fingers; and express themselves. Hears name. ii) Shows awareness of hearing own name, and of multi-sensory resources.	Opportunities provided for experimenting with multi-sensory activities on an individual basis.	
P2	i) Responds to multi-sensory experiences by moving hands, responds to name. ii) Recognises familiar people and objects, begins to move hands in different media to explore.	1:1 work with adult to encourage response, giving praise where movements are appropriate.	
P3	i) Explores media in more complex ways, moving fingers and hands to elicit response. ii) Anticipates different textures and temperatures. Anticipates name being called during registration.	Multi-sensory activities in whole class or 1:1 to explore in sand, paint. Registration. Hello games.	
P4	Makes marks with large simple tools. Understands that marks and symbols have meaning. Uses cause/effect to press a switch meaningfully.	Name cards. Daily practise of hearing and writing in the air as well as with simple tools. Simple ICT switch programmes.	
P5	Colours own name card. Finds own name card among others. Traces over name. Writes initial letter of own name independently.	Daily practise of tracing. Writing initial sound.	

Suggested books, other resources
Range of sensory resources eg sand/paint.
Large pens/pencils/crayons/brushes.
Name cards. Letter cards.

TEXT LEVEL: WRITING: COMPOSITION

T.L. YR: LO 12.2 *cont.*

Through guided and independent writing to write their own names.

See also: Section 1.5; 2.4 Refer to Section 1, no 5; Section 2, no 4

Steps	Learning Objectives/Targets	Activities/Strategies	Resources
P6	Begins to write initial letter of own name. Copies name and begins to produce a recognisable initial letter.	Daily practise of name writing using pens, paints, tracing, sand, pens.	
P7	Holds large pencil accurately. Forms many letters correctly.	As above, ensuring good models and correct orientation of letters and practise surname.	
P8	Writes own first name using large pencil with initial letter accurate and others recognisable. Writes full name in many different ways and for many different purposes.	As above.	

Suggested books, other resources
Range of sensory resources, e.g. sand/paint.
Large pens/pencils/crayons/brushes.
Name cards. Letter cards.

TEXT LEVEL: WRITING: COMPOSITION

T.L. YR: LO 12.3

Through guided and independent writing to write labels or captions for pictures and drawings.

Steps	Learning Objectives/Targets	Activities/Strategies	Resources
P1–3	Following LO 12.2. Encounters and experiences and has opportunities to explore and respond by looking and touching a range of objects with labels on.	Whole class sessions in which teacher indicates objects with labels and helps pupils to look and touch, read and identify.	
P4	Shows interest in objects and an awareness that objects are constant.	Whole class sessions in which pupils and adults discuss naming of objects in books and class.	
P5	Matches objects to pictures/words/symbols in classroom. Draws and adult labels drawing.	Matching games with objects. Painting/drawing with adult writing captions.	
P6	Recognises many objects and watches as adult writes labels for them. Draws own pictures for adult to write captions. Copies/traces written captions/labels.	Pupils draw pictures of own news or story. Teacher writes caption which pupils copy, trace or use IT.	Adult support.
P7	Identifies labels or captions. Helps adult to write captions in shared text and writing times. Begins to write own words to describe own drawings.	Word cards, independent news times.	Word cards.
P8	Uses words and sentences independently in own news or diary. Makes suggestions of captions for class shared writing. Uses simple dictionary.	Pupils use own word books in alphabetical order to write labels, captions or news.	Simple word books in alphabetical order.
			Range of simple dictionaries.
			As above.

Suggested books, other resources
Picture/object matching. Identification of initial sound. Own word books to help complete (b all). Class alphabet books, charts, etc.
My First Amazing Dictionary: Dorling Kindersley.
Class Alphabet Books/charts.
Pupils' word books. Pictures and objects. Word cards/captions. Letter cards.

TEXT LEVEL: WRITING: COMPOSITION

T.L. YR: LO 12.4

Through guided and independent writing to write sentences to match pictures or sequence of pictures.

Steps	Learning Objectives/Targets	Activities/Strategies	Resources
P1–5	Build on activities from LO 12.3.		
P6	Uses words and simple print or signs to describe a given picture or sequence of pictures with support.	In small groups pupils use words to describe a picture or each picture in a sequence. Adult scribes.	
P7	Matches printed words and syllables to given picture or sequence of pictures. Begins to write captions with support.	Matching activity. Pupils match words or sequences of pictures to simple sentences and trace over and read sentences.	
P8	Writes simple sentences to match pictures and builds up to a sequence of pictures and captions to identify some words to use to write sentences.	Teacher provides picture or photograph. In small groups pupils suggest words to use and try to find them on word cards or in simple dictionaries and write them down.	Word cards. Simple dictionaries.

Suggested books, other resources
Clicker with appropriate ready made or self made grid: Crick.
All about you by Catherine and Laurence Anholt. Pub: Mammoth. ISBN 07497 1297 X.
Noah and The Rabbits by Sally Kilroy. Pub: Puffin. ISBN 0-14-054346-5.
Sequenced pictures. Word cards. Pupil news. Prepared story cards.

TEXT LEVEL: WRITING: COMPOSITION

T.L. YR: LO 12.5

Through guided and independent writing to experiment with writing and recognise how their own version matches and differs from conventional version.

Steps	Learning Objectives/Targets	Activities/Strategies	Resources
P1–5	As LO 12.1, 12.2, 12.3, 12.4.		
P6	Recognises that there is a difference between their own version of a story and the conventional one.	Adult reads conventional story enabling pupils to see text. They write own versions using words/sentences and recognise differences. Pupils talk about what happens.	
P7	Joins in with re-telling stories in own words. Writes same story using words and sentences.	Pupils take turns to re-tell story (above). Discussion about different ways of telling and writing story.	
P8	Knows that own version of story, both told and written, is different from conventional version. To use sequence of pictures to re-tell familiar story.	Pupils work independently to sequence pictures of story, and sentences, and compare finished sequences and discuss differences.	

Suggested books, other resources
Sequenced pictures. Word cards. Pre-prepared story cards.

TEXT LEVEL: WRITING: COMPOSITION

T.L. YR: LO 13

To think about and discuss what they intend to write ahead of writing it.

Steps	Learning Objectives/Targets	Activities/Strategies	Resources
P1–3	Encounters and experiences and has opportunities to respond to shared pictures, stories and rhymes and discussion about everyday activities, i.e. news time.	Adults and pupils share stories and pictures and discuss pupils' activities at home and at school.	
P4	Shows interest in writing stories as they work as part of a whole class shared time and discuss how to make up a story/messages/letters.	Teacher and pupil share writing a story/letter/message and discuss.	
P5	Begins to think about and say what they want to write, talk about their own news.	Teacher uses 'news' with flip chart and asks the pupils what their news is and scribes.	
P6	Talks about the sequence of their story or news, e.g. first this then this.	Individually pupil talks about a story or account and what they want to write. Adult scribes.	
P7	Join in with drafting a story before writing it.	With an adult pupil lists/makes simple draft of what they intend. Adult scribes with pupil's help.	
P8	Plans a story with beginning, middle and end.	Pupil discusses story with adult, talking about beginning, middle and end. Adult scribes with pupil's help.	

Suggested books, other resources
News times. Use of flip charts/photos/objects. Lists of words/simple dictionaries. Teacher scribes where necessary.
Simple tape recorder or Dictaphone.
Pictures/photographs/objects. Lists of words/word cards.

TEXT LEVEL: WRITING: COMPOSITION

T.L. YR: LO 14

To use experience of stories, poems and simple recounts as a basis for independent writing.

Steps	Learning Objectives/Targets	Activities/Strategies	Resources
P1–3	Encounters and experiences and has opportunities to respond to stories, poems and simple rhymes, particularly familiar ones.	Teacher reads or tells a wide range of familiar stories and rhymes.	
P4	Begins to help with re-telling by adding a word, sign or sound.	Encourage pupils in whole groups to vocalise their own responses to appropriate parts.	
P5	Re-tells familiar stories verbally, with vocalisation or gestures.	Teacher tells or reads a familiar story. Pupils re-tell part of this.	
P6	Re-tells part of a familiar story using pictures and captions or puppets.	Using pictures, captions or puppets, each pupil completes one part of a familiar story. With teacher, it is put together in sequence to make a story book.	
P7	Re-tells a familiar story using pictures and captions and simple sentences.	Working individually with adult pupil completes each picture and caption and sequences them to re-write the story.	
P8	Makes a first draft from original plan using simple sentences.	Opportunities for pupil to write beginning, middle and end of familiar story.	

Suggested books, other resources
Use simple poem or rhymes to support own writing. Group story telling – each pupil re-tells/chooses picture to complete part of story. Adult scribes.
Clicker with appropriate ready made or self made grid: Crick.
The Enormous Turnip, re-told by Mary Shepherd. Pub: Collins. Resource pack 0 0031 3952 2.
* *Ben's Baby* by Michael Foreman. Pub: Collins. Resource pack 0 00 313953 0.
Pictures, captions and/or puppets representing characters.

111

TEXT LEVEL: WRITING: COMPOSITION

T.L. YR: LO 15

To use writing to communicate in a variety of ways, incorporating it into play and everyday classroom life.

Steps	Learning Objectives/Targets	Activities/Strategies	Resources
P1–3	Encounters and experiences and has opportunities to respond to use of writing of words/symbols to convey meaning, e.g. names, date, weather.	Daily communication activities such as registration times, daily structure and tasks.	
P4	Recognises objects/symbols around the classroom of tasks for the day.	Teacher provides 'daily tasks' using words and symbols. With class, teacher goes through these tasks, indicating words/symbols.	
P5	Makes timetable/list/menu using play writing or computer or symbols.	All pupils to make own timetable through picture, word or symbol using play writing with pencil or computer. Teacher goes through individual tasks with each pupil.	
P6	Draws and play writes as part of everyday play situations, e.g. post office, letters to friends, letters home.	Pupils make greetings card and send message using their own drawing and writing.	
P7	Uses drawing and writing in everyday classroom activities.	Pupils use word cards to write menus for play house or cooking. Pupils identify items for lunches or cooking and write shopping lists using words, symbols or pictures.	
P8	Records tasks completed in the classroom.	Pupils fill in given assessment charts or tick lists of tasks completed.	

Suggested books, other resources
Making Christmas cards/birthday cards. Writing a home/school diary, i.e. drawing or finding picture/symbol to be stuck in. Taking written messages. Pen-friends. *Talk Write Away*: Black Cat.
Words/symbols of daily tasks. Word/symbols cards or pictures for food/shopping. Lists of tasks or assessment charts.
Pictures, captions and/or puppets representing characters.

An example of how the KS3 strategy materials can be adapted to provide a more age appropriate approach to delivering those earlier objectives

Pupils at Key Stage 3 may still need to work from objectives from earlier years. Pupils with severe and complex needs, may indeed still be working on the Reception Year objectives. The main overriding issue is to ensure that whatever level they are working towards, they have entitlement to the broad curriculum offered to their more able peers. The framework for Key Stage 3 extends the word, sentence and text level organisation of the primary framework, and includes speaking and listening, and drama.

Catch-up unit for pupils in Year 7 who are working at level 3 and below are being produced by the Standards and Effectiveness Unit by the end of 2001. These will provide flexible and practical methods of catching up for pupils out of step with others of the same age. Pupils working at the very earliest levels, may need to use the small steps approach included in this book. This will help pupils to build on prior skills so that good foundations are formed. If pupils are working alongside their peer group, it may be that they will need to 'explore and respond' to age-appropriate experiences offered, at their own level.

Pupils in Years 7–9 who are working at a Pre level 1 stage should:
Have access to texts appropriate to age as illustrated in the case study materials in Part 2.

In line with recommendations in the KS3 NLS Framework they should also have access to age-appropriate content for pupils at KS3. For example:

Y7 *Speaking*: Pupils should have the opportunity to:
- Experience and respond to stories, instructions, points of view, talks, presentations, in a wide range of differing opportunities.

Y7 *Listening*: Pupils should have the opportunity to:
- Experience and respond to a range of activities in which they hear discussion, answer questions, listen to stories and intimations, recall messages and reflect on what they have heard.

Y7 *Drama*: Pupils should have the opportunity to:
- Experience and respond to a range of drama techniques in a variety of ways such as role play, facial expression, body language, anticipation, scripted and unscripted plays, characters, relationships.

Some examples of these are given on the following pages.

TEXT LEVEL: DRAMA

Through a range of drama techniques pupils will seek to achieve the following Learning Objectives/Targets

Steps	Learning Objectives/Targets	Activities/Strategies	Resources
P 1	i) Experiences and encounters a range of role play situations so that differing viewpoints are established. ii) Shows awareness of above activity.	Involvement in range of role play. Adult models and encourages facial and body expressions. Interactive games.	
P 2	i) Responds to different roles as they play a part in role play. ii) Recognises that different expressions, volume, style are used for effect.	Begins to take part with peers and benefits from watching different pupils take different roles. Tries to make different facial expressions. Responds to them in others.	
P 3	i) Participates in some way with above activities. ii) Anticipates their own turn in a role play situation.	Opportunities to participate in whole class activities are provided with encouragement by adult, allowing time for response. Some peer partnerships.	
P 4	Shows interest in other people's points of view, and begins to work collaboratively.	Opportunities to work in small groups discussing a particular point of view and work to present it to others. Peer partners.	
P 5	Follows the simple drama or role play activities, offering some contribution. Develops own performance of facial/body language.	Involvement in simple unscripted portrayals of characters, feelings or aspects of simple script. Explore improvements in expression and facial or body movements with adult help.	
P 6	Works with others to present simple drama, expressions, roles.	Developing opportunities for pupils to work together to improve and portray a role in told or read story.	

TEXT LEVEL: DRAMA *cont.*

Through a range of drama techniques pupils will seek to achieve the following Learning Objectives/Targets

Steps	Learning Objectives/Targets	Activities/Strategies	Resources
P7	Works with others to improve performance, reflecting on and commenting on it.	Opportunities to reflect. Taking video perhaps of prior performances and discussing and improving.	
P8	Begins to solve simple problems linked to scripted and unscripted dramas.	Opportunities to think about different roles and find solutions. Peer groups partners.	

Suggested books, other resources
The following have been adapted by teachers to provide age-appropriate contexts for pupils working on the P levels:
Macbeth – Shakespeare (and others).
Oliver Twist – Charles Dickens.
Character studies from different age-appropriate stories.
Mood observations and demonstrations. Simplified Story Version of Shakespeare from Cutting Edge Publications, Lostwithiel, Cornwall. (Tel: 01208 872337)

TEXT LEVEL: SPEAKING AND LISTENING

Through a range of speaking and listening experiences pupils will seek to achieve the following Learning Objectives/Targets

Steps	Learning Objectives/Targets	Activities/Strategies	Resources
7S 1	i) Encounters and experiences a range of stories, instructions, expositions, explorations, points of views and arguments. ii) Shows awareness of the above experiences by movement/eye contact.	Whole class participate in range of discussion, stories, expositions, and news, etc. Pupil experiences, responds to and begins to follow and show awareness of speaker.	
S2	i) Responds to stories, instructions, expositions, explorations, points of views and arguments consistently. ii) Cooperates and recognises when different people are talking in the above context and begins to listen.	Wide range of different types of text and spoken language to encourage eye contact, and awareness of different speakers and contexts. Multi-media news item.	
S3	i) Participates in the activities by focusing on speaking and following. ii) Anticipates who will speak next.	Involvement in group activities in which they benefit from peer modelling, adult encourages interaction. School council activities.	
S4	Shows interest in aspects of the discussion, turning head to listen better.	Simple prompts to encourage interaction. Range of multi-media stories/expositions.	
S5	Begins to follow aspects of story, instructions, expositions and tries to join in appropriately.	As above, increase opportunities to share and talk about different points of view.	
S6	Follows a simple story, instruction, explanation, point of view and contributes in some way. Taking turns in conversation.	Adult may need to give a chance of two opposing points and ask 'This one . . . or this one?' Adult encourages and prompts.	
S7	Join in at appropriate time in above activities, and reflects on discussion.	Opportunities to reflect on and contribute to arguments and different points of view.	
S8	Is aware of different parts of stories and instructions, and different points of view, contributing as appropriate.	Thinking time given. Opportunities to offer own view point about an item that interests them.	

Suggested books, other resources
The following have been adapted by teachers to provide age-appropriate contexts for pupils working on the P levels:
Diary of Anne Frank – extracts.
Aesop's Fables.
Health leaflets and posters from Smallwood Publishing Group, The Old Bakery, Charlton House, Dour Street, Dover. smallwood.co.uk
World War 2 Anthology, Poetry. Big Book, Pelican.